Thank you so much for your support & prayers for Myanmar! On behalf of our team,
Allison & Paul ☺

DESERT RIVER

True Stories of Pain and Provision in Myanmar

Edited By:

Su L. N.
Nay Dar
K. T. Par
N. San
Soon Tar Ni
Lian Sandy
Allison McKnight
Kalina Davis

Copyright ©2024 by Su L. N., Nay Dar, K. T. Par, N. San, Soon Tar Ni, Lian Sandy, Allison McKnight, and Kalina Davis.

All rights reserved. No portion of this book may be reproduced in any form without written permission from the publisher or author, except as permitted by U.S. copyright law.

All Scripture quotations, unless otherwise indicated, are taken from the Holy Bible, New International Version®, NIV®. Copyright ©1973, 1978, 1984, 2011 by Biblica, Inc.™ All rights reserved worldwide. www.zondervan.com. The "NIV" and "New International Version" are trademarks registered in the United States Patent and Trademark Office by Biblica, Inc.™

ISBN: 979-8-9898656-0-4

Some names and locations have been changed.

Cover and book design by Tais Lemos Hale.

Printed in the United States of America.

First printing, 2024.

Behold, I am doing a new thing; now it springs forth, do you not perceive it? I will make a way in the wilderness and rivers in the desert.

—Isaiah 43:19 (ESV)

CONTENTS

Notes Of Gratitude From Our Myanmar Board 8

Acknowledgments 10

PREFACE   13

INTRODUCTION   19

SCORCHED   31

    Running 34

    Quench 36

    Shade 40

    Oasis 48

    Channel 52

    Swell 54

PARCHED   63

    Fish 66

    Clear 70

    Immerse 72

    Refresh 78

    Revive 80

    Covered 82

DUNES   91

    Rapids 94

    Rivulet 98

    Convergence 102

    Spring 106

    Ebb 112

    Deep 114

    Steady 116

WILDERNESS — 123
- Drop 126
- Thirst 130

CANYON — 139
- Current 142
- Flood 148
- Saturate 150
- Eddy 154
- Flow 156
- Ripples 158
- Wellspring 162

EDGES — 169
- Torrent 172
- Submerge 174
- Deluge 176
- Parted 180
- Lifeline 184
- Waterfall 186
- Everflow 192

DELTA — 203
- Rain 206
- Cascade 210

CONCLUSION — 219
WHAT'S NEXT? — 223
ABOUT THE TEAM — 226

Notes Of Gratitude From Our Myanmar Board

I would like to appreciate and acknowledge every individual who shared their own stories and personal experiences to reflect the current situation of Myanmar and how God is working with us.

—Nay Dar

I would like to thank God first. Also, thanks to Allison and Kalina, who worked really hard to be able to publish the book in North America, and to all of our board members and authors, who did their best to make this happen.

—K. T. Par

I would like to thank our authors who have contributed to this book. Your stories serve as a powerful reminder of God's faithfulness and goodness, and the reminder that God is still working even when we are surrounded by darkness. I would also like to thank the readers of this book. May you find comfort, hope, and encouragement as you reflect on these stories and continue on your own faith journey. To God, I thank you for your guidance throughout this process. We offer this book to you as a gift of worship.

—Soon Tar Ni

I would like to thank God for giving me the opportunity to take part in compiling this book. During the pandemic and throughout the ongoing military violence, I have felt discouraged and sometimes depressed. However, because God gave me the opportunity to participate in this project, I feel like I can still help others. That has been a real encouragement to me. May this book be a blessing to you as well.

—N. San

First of all, I would like to thank God who has blessed and led us in starting and completing this amazing book. I would like to thank each of you who shared and testified about the goodness of God, faithfulness of God, guidance, and love of God that you experienced in your own life so that others can regain strength in their lives and be encouraged through these stories. Thank you so much to each of our board members who actively and willingly helped to make this book. I would also like to express our gratitude to the readers of this book. I believe that you will feel and see how God is good and faithful in our lives after you read this book. After reading this book, I also pray that you will be able to share the goodness of God with others. Thank you so much everyone, and God bless you all.

—Su L. N.

I am deeply grateful to those who shared their stories as well as to everyone who contributed to the completion of this book. The authors' testimonies reveal the unwavering faith of our people—finding a "desert river"—even during times of hardship. It showcases how God consistently stands by his sons and daughters!

—Lian Sandy

Acknowledgments

So many things need to come together for a book to make it into a reader's hands. We would like to express our gratitude to each and every person who made the sharing of these stories possible. Thank you from the bottom of our hearts to our dear authors, who had the courage to share their stories and felt compelled to encourage others with what they have seen God do in their lives. Thank you for taking time to answer questions and provide clarifying information, and for giving us your permission to share your stories. Thank you for the ways you are holding onto God at this terrible time, which continues to provide profound inspiration to others.

Thank you to our translators who took the time to type and translate, to clarify, and to check and recheck the stories that were submitted. Thank you to our multiethnic, Myanmar-national board members for this book: Su L. N., Nay Dar, K. T. Par, N. San, Soon Tar Ni, and Lian Sandy, who spent mornings and evenings in meetings and deliberations, collected testimonies, and provided direction, input, and wise decisions. Board members connected with the authors over a period of three months, culminating in hours of in-person meetings and phone conversations.[1] We are so grateful for their time and emotional commitment throughout this process.

Thank you to our donors who allowed for this book to be professionally edited and designed through their generous contribution of funds. Thank you Samaritan's Purse Canada for your ongoing support to projects in Myanmar that deliver physical and spiritual aid to those in crisis. Thank you Jason Martens and Bruce Piercey for your time and commitment, for hearing our vision, and for enabling us to see it come to life. We thank our developmental and copyeditor, Mariah Gumpert, and

---

1 *Story collection was guided by ethical storytelling principles including supporting the agency and autonomy of the authors in how their stories were told and presented.*

our graphic designer, Tais Lemos Hale, for your hard work and patience throughout the process. Thank you to Fiona Cheng for your kind consultations on mood boards and design ideation, to Felicity Davis for your meticulous copyediting and proofreading, to Tamara Wee for your incredibly detailed file review, and to our beta readers Tom Opdyke, Rachel C. Kettle, Anna Meinecke, Linda Bennet, and Manuel Mangahas, for your time and thoughtful feedback on our manuscript. We thank our family and friends and our church networks for listening (and relistening) to this vision and supporting us in spreading the word about this book.

We also thank the courageous individuals and organizations who are on the front lines in Myanmar, helping displaced communities and those impacted by war. From money transfers and coordination to purchasing, transporting, and distributing aid, we know that each part includes its own risks and challenges that can have devastating impacts on your and/or your family's safety. We thank you for your courage, hard work, and relentless motivation to assist those in need.

Thank you, reader, for purchasing and valuing the precious book in your hands. In turn, please be assured that every effort will be made for the book's proceeds to arrive in the hands of those who need it most—whether it be in the form of food, medicine, shelter, or other supplies.

Most of all, we thank you, God. This book is a response to Psalm 96:3: "Publish his glorious deeds among the nations. Tell everyone about the amazing things he does" (NLT). Without you, God, there is no hope. Throughout history, it has become painfully clear that there are no economic, political, or social systems that can save us from ourselves. Because we are fallible, our solutions are fallible. All of our grand theories, striving, and intellectual posturing—they run their course and come to nothing without you. Thank you for never giving up on us. Thank you for how you are moving.

PREFACE

Why Read This Book?

The stories in this book are true—so true that at times our minds may want to make them untrue, to make them a work of fiction or take comfort in the physical, cultural, and political distance that separates us from the storytellers. We challenge you, dear reader, to resist disassociating from these stories. Do not read them as if you were watching a movie, or as if you were in a car with the scenery flying by. Receive them as you would a close friend recounting a personal experience, giving their precious time and emotional energy to provide a window into their heart. Be in wonder and awe with us at the authors' praise for God—and continued spiritual perseverance—even when there seems to be so much to despair. Try to see what they see and feel how they feel.

Follow them to a desert river.

In reality, there are sounds, smells, overwhelming emotions, and layered connotations packed behind many of the words used in these stories. For example, a writer may assume that you would implicitly understand the panic, mind-blanking chaos, and confusion associated with the phrase "run away." This includes the jarring, uncompromising sounds of gunfire and the cold dread of screaming fighter planes. It includes the exhaustion, the uncertainty, the jungle with monsoon rains dripping into your bones, the clouds of relentless mosquitoes and the wet dirt floor. Likewise, a writer may assume you are familiar with the horror, outrage, and endless accounts of torture and violence associated with the word "military." They may think you will subconsciously remember the continued use of civilians as human shields, the burning alive of women and children, and the posting of the bodies of resistance fighters on state media. They may assume you will understand the impossibility of reasoning with military soldiers on the basis of ethics or humanity or law, making any interaction with them a dangerous and unpredictable endeavor. Because of this, we seek to take moments between accounts to unpack the layers of context for you through personal statements, poems, and both visual and cognitive space so that the implications of these words charged with memories, stories, and emotions can be illuminated in some way. We've also included quotes from Myanmar believers that depict their incredible faith and spiritual perseverance. We find this necessary to accurately convey the beautiful words and hearts of the writers, which stand out in stark relief to the oftentimes bleak situation that surrounds them.

Through their stories, the authors claim that they have experienced a "desert river"—a place of God-shaped life, growth, and change in the midst of desolation. This term is taken from Isaiah 43:19, which says, "Behold, I am doing a new thing; now it springs forth, do you not perceive it? I will make a way in the wilderness and rivers in the desert" (ESV). It's hard to believe that one can experience life and provision in the face of tragedy and overwhelming destruction. And yet, these authors claim that they have seen it, that they have been to the water's edge. They claim that a desert river is there even when sight, smell, taste, and touch declare it is not.

Their stories, at times, may challenge us. Their statements of faith may even feel trite, oversimplified, or inauthentic to a Western reader concerned with complexity, nuance, and critique.

We assure you that these Myanmar authors are no strangers to complexity. They are no strangers to real loss, pain, and heartache—and they do not deny that those feelings are there. They do not need to be reminded of what life is really like or how difficult it can be.

Instead, there is a profound beauty in the simplicity, in the loyalty, in the commitment that they are focused on, that they aspire to. There is a depth to their fidelity that can be dismissed if we do not pause to hold it with sincere regard.

Let the stories of these Myanmar authors minister to you and settle deep into your soul. Let their clarity inspire you and not deter you. Let us humble our hearts to learn from them and receive with gratitude what they have to give.

The objectives of this book are fourfold:

- First, to give God glory and praise for creating desert rivers in the midst of violence and chaos in Myanmar
- Second, to provide encouragement to readers in the West and East with stories of his goodness and the perseverance of the faith of believers in Myanmar
- Third, to raise awareness about what is happening in Myanmar and the incredible need there, as it is rarely covered in international media
- Finally, to raise funds through the purchase of the book to send back to Myanmar in support of humanitarian assistance

This book also offers readers an opportunity to engage in prayer for our brothers and sisters in Myanmar, while also giving space for personal and spiritual reflection. We find this particularly meaningful, as it provides a beautiful response to our Myanmar authors who have gifted their stories as a ministry of encouragement to you, the reader.

Not all of the stories shared in this book take place in the present time of armed conflict—just as in the psalms, some of our writers have chosen to reflect on the past in order to face the present, reminding themselves of how God has moved in challenging times and how he can do it again. These stories also reflect on God's presence in their ordinary lives before the crisis began, whether during school exams, struggling with health, or facing challenging situations at work. The authors use these past reminders of God's faithfulness to strengthen themselves in the midst of the current crisis. Others have chosen to write an expression of grief and distress—a lament—bringing all that they have to the One in the midst of pain, anger, confusion, and unanswered prayers. These entries are honest, raw, and sorrowful—yet worshipful—in their recognition and reach for a God that has the power and love to save, in the painful space of waiting.

It may go without saying that the identities of the writers and any compromising information, including the names of locations, organizations, and affiliations, have been removed or replaced with pseudonyms for the writers' safety and protection. The quotes from Myanmar nationals throughout this book are likewise unattributed. Our authors and contributors hail from a wide spectrum of denominational backgrounds, and therefore there is rich variety in their experiences and the articulation of those experiences. This book is not intended as a theological exposition or a critical analysis but rather an offering of worship to God, from Christians across Myanmar.

For readers who feel inspired to take further action, we have included a section at the end of the book for ideas on how to spiritually, financially, and socially partner with communities in Myanmar.

To provide additional context to the stories, we begin with a cursory (and necessarily incomplete) summary of Myanmar's current crisis.

INTRODUCTION
What is Happening in Myanmar?

A Brief History

Myanmar (also known as "Burma") is no stranger to military conquest and dictatorship.[1] Colonized by the British in the nineteenth century, Myanmar was subjected to decades of foreign military occupation. Since the dawn of its restoration to independence in 1948, it has felt the impact of a military elite grappling for control and power.

Myanmar is rich in natural resources of teak, gas, jade, and gems, and couched in a geographically significant position, flanked by India to the west and China to the east. More than 60 percent of its workforce is employed in the agriculture sector.[2] In the latest census, almost 90 percent of the population were reported to be Buddhist, while only 6 percent were reported as Christian.[3]

Myanmar is comprised of fourteen states and divisions, which are home to well over a hundred different ethnicities aside from the Bamar ethnic majority. A number of these ethnic groups have maintained their own armed organizations, formed to defend their lands and people against encroaching Bamar soldiers, in what has been considered "one of the longest and most complex

---

1 *While "Burma" was the name given by the British during colonial rule, the country's name was changed to "Myanmar" by the military regime in 1989. Neither name is representative of all ethnicities in the country, as both make reference to the majority ethnic group, the Bamar ("Myanmar" is the formal written term; "Burma" is the spoken term). In diplomatic circles, most nation-states have adopted the use of "Myanmar" while others (such as the United States and United Kingdom) continue to use "Burma" in objection to the military regime. We use the term "Myanmar" in this book in following the practice of our national authors and editors, though we acknowledge that neither term is ideal.* Andrew Selth and Adam Gallagher, "What's in a Name: Burma or Myanmar? A Decision by the U.S. to Accept the Name Myanmar Seems Unlikely Any Time Soon," *United States Institute of Peace Blog*, June 21, 2018, https://www.usip.org/blog/2018/06/whats-name-burma-or-myanmar.

2 Sergiy Zorya, "Unleashing Myanmar's Agricultural Potential," World Bank Blogs, May 27, 2016, https://blogs.worldbank.org/eastasiapacific/unleashing-myanmar-agricultural-potential.

3 The Republic of the Union of Myanmar, "The 2014 Myanmar Population and Housing Census, The Union Report: Religion, Census Report Volume 2-C", Ministry of Labour, Immigration and Population, Department of Population, Myanmar, July 2016 https://myanmar.unfpa.org/sites/default/files/pub-pdf/UNION_2C_Religion_EN.pdf.

civil wars in the world."[4] For example, one of the largest ethnic organizations, the Karen National Union (KNU), has been at war with the Myanmar military for over seventy years. As such, not all areas in Myanmar are considered "government-controlled," as ethnic groups control their own administration and governance in certain territories.

Protests and demonstrations for democratic reforms have happened throughout the country, culminating in violent military crackdowns during the widespread student-led protests of 1988 and 1996 and during the 2007 Saffron Revolution. Aung San Suu Kyi, a political activist and stalwart campaigner for democracy, made international headlines after being under house arrest for years as the leader of the National League for Democracy (NLD). Her party won a landslide victory in the 1990 election, but their success was denied as the military government refused to recognize the results.

In 2011, Myanmar started to increase its economic, political, and social engagement with the world. Under a thinly veiled pretense of democracy, military elites adopted the appearance of civilian politicians. However, both national and international critics still contended that elections were neither free nor fair.[5]

Finally, in 2015, an election was held with another landslide victory for the NLD, and this time the results were upheld with the NLD taking office in 2016. It seemed that Myanmar had entered a new era, one of hope and progress. However, underneath the surface of triumph and optimism, observers recognized that due to

---

[4] World Bank Group, "Myanmar: Economic Transition amid Conflict; A Systematic Country Diagnostic," World Bank, November 25, 2019, 2, https://www.worldbank.org/en/country/myanmar/publication/myanmar-economic-transition-amid-conflict-a-systematic-country-diagnostic.

[5] "Burma: By-Elections a Step, but Not Real Reform," Human Rights Watch, March 30, 2012, https://www.hrw.org/news/2012/03/30/burma-elections-step-not-real-reform; "History of Elections in Myanmar," Myanmar Election Watch, https://myanmarelectionwatch.org/en/history-of-elections-in-myanmar, accessed August 16, 2023.

the amended 2008 constitution, the military had positioned itself for guaranteed control and power, whether directly or indirectly.[6]

The NLD's transition into positions of government administration and leadership was not an easy one. The military's amended constitution in 2008 had given it an automatic 25 percent of seats in parliament, manifesting as the power to veto any decisions or changes it did not agree with. The military also acted independently of the NLD government and continued to control an incredible scope of economic interests in Myanmar.

Many of the nation's ethnic groups still did not feel that the NLD was representing their concerns, and Myanmar military attacks continued against ethnic groups and communities including the Kachin, Shan, Karen, and others, even under the newly formed nationwide cease-fire agreement. Forced displacement of the Rohingya from violence in Rakhine State happened in 1978, 1992, 2012, and 2016, with by far the largest forced displacement beginning in August 2017 and culminating to nearly one million Rohingya people forced to flee their homes since.[7] A United Nations fact-finding mission found such overwhelming

---

[6] Vikram Nehru, "Myanmar's Military Keeps Firm Grip on Democratic Transition," Carnegie Endowment for International Peace, June 2, 2015, https://carnegieendowment.org/2015/06/02/myanmar-s-military-keeps-firm-grip-on-democratic-transition-pub-60288.

[7] *As of September 30, 2022, over 940,000 Rohingya refugees have been registered in Bangladesh, residing in extremely challenging environments of Cox's Bazar District and the island of Bhasan Char.* "Joint Response Plan Rohingya Humanitarian Crisis January–December 2023," United Nations Office for the Coordination of Humanitarian Affairs (OCHA), 14, accessed October 12, 2023, https://www.humanitarianresponse.info/en/operations/bangladesh/document/bangladesh-2023-joint-response-plan-rohingya-humanitarian-crisis.

evidence of extreme violence that they made recommendations to investigate and prosecute senior generals of the Myanmar military "for genocide, crimes against humanity and war crimes."[8] This ongoing violence, even under the auspices of the NLD, highlighted a long-standing rift between ethnic groups in the country and the central Bamar-majority government.

Current Conflict

After the NLD's first five-year term of governance, elections were again due to be held, and the NLD administration, though clearly imperfect, was reelected. However, on February 1, 2021, the military staged a coup and imprisoned elected government leaders, citing election fraud. These claims were seen as unfounded, and hundreds of thousands of civilians across the nation took to the streets in peaceful protest, demanding restoration of lawfully elected government officials. Thousands of government officials, teachers, medical staff, and others employed in public service positions refused to work under the military apparatus as part of a "civil disobedience movement" (CDM). A shadow government was formed, the National Unity Government (NUG), claiming legal legitimacy. A deadly tailspin began when the military responded violently.

Since then, ethnic armies and newly formed people's defense forces have come into daily armed clashes with a Myanmar military seeking to stamp out any resistance to its authority

---

8 *The 2018 United Nations fact-finding mission determined that crimes against humanity and war crimes have been committed in Kachin, Shan, and Rakhine States by the Myanmar military since 2011. In Rakhine State, additional crimes of apartheid and persecution of the Rohingya, characterized by extermination and deportation, were found.* "Report of the Independent Fact-Finding Mission on Myanmar," Human Rights Council, September 10–28, 2018, A/HRC/39/64, paragraph 88, 105, https://digitallibrary.un.org/record/1648304?ln=en; Simon Lewis and Humeyra Pamuk, "Blinken Says Myanmar Army Committed Genocide in 'Widespread and Systematic' Attacks on Rohingya," Reuters, March 22, 2022, https://www.reuters.com/world/china/blinken-says-us-determined-myanmar-army-committed-genocide-against-rohingya-2022-03-21/.

and control.⁹ While ethnic armies have intimate knowledge and navigation of the land, the Myanmar military has invaded the air—and the corresponding earth—with fighter jets, missiles, bombs, and helicopters.

At the time of writing, over 2.3 million Myanmar civilians have been forced to flee their homes due to military attacks and ongoing violence.¹⁰ More than 4,500 people have been killed, and over 26,000 people have been arrested, charged, or sentenced since the start of the coup. A total of 78,737 homes have been burned down since May 1, 2021.¹¹ In 2022 alone, there were 312 incidents of air and drone strikes, outside of battle, with each incident including multiple air strikes.¹² Experts agree that the exponential increase in land mine casualties in Myanmar is the largest ever recorded.¹³ An estimated 17.6 million people are currently in need of humanitarian assistance.¹⁴

---

9 *"Ethnic armies" or "ethnic armed groups" are a formalized military within certain ethnic groups in the country. Other terms used for these groups, to varying degrees of preference, include "ethnic armed organization," "ethnic resistance group," and "ethnic resistance organization."*

10 "Myanmar Humanitarian Update No. 35 (as of 12 January 2024)," United Nations Office for the Coordination of Humanitarian Affairs (OCHA), January 12, 2024, https://myanmar.un.org/en/257739-myanmar-humanitarian-update-no-35. *Note that when combined with pre-coup displacement numbers, a total of over 2.6 million people are now displaced within Myanmar.*

11 "Daily Briefing in Relation to the Military Coup," Assistance Association for Political Prisoners (Burma), February 16, 2024, https://aappb.org/?p=27438; "Incident Map: Number of Houses Burned Down by Myanmar's Military (1 May 2021 to 31 December 2023)," Data for Myanmar, January 20, 2024, https://www.datawrapper.de/_/ci4tH/.

12 Rebecca Ratcliffe and Min Ye Kyaw, "'Monster from the Sky': Two Years on from Coup, Myanmar Junta Increases Airstrikes on Civilians," *Guardian*, January 31, 2023, https://www.theguardian.com/world/2023/jan/31/monster-from-the-sky-two-years-on-from-coup-myanmar-junta-increases-airstrikes-on-civilians.

13 Victoria Milko and David Rising, "'I Just Want My Legs Back': Myanmar Landmine Casualties Soar," Associated Press, February 19, 2023, https://apnews.com/article/myanmar-government-china-0451f807790016c8e46114bb01441fe4.

14 Zaheena Rasheed and Nu Nu Lusan, "Charred Bodies, Burned Homes: A 'Campaign of Terror' in Myanmar," Al Jazeera, May 12, 2023, https://www.aljazeera.com/news/longform/2023/5/12/charred-bodies-burned-homes-a-campaign-of-terror-in-myanmar-2.

There are rumors that at the beginning of the current conflict, military leader Min Aung Hlaing received dark spiritual divination. Among the astrological guidance provided, Min Aung Hlaing was advised to start shooting protesters in the head to secure success. It was reported that many protesters in the early stages of the conflict were indeed killed by head shots.[15]

Correlated or not, it becomes increasingly hard to comprehend and explain the military's cruel and excessive use of violence without invoking the word evil. How else is it possible to characterize the torture and indiscriminate killing of civilians, of dismemberment, of rape, of burning entire villages to the ground, of the casual dismissing of horror and outrage that communities have expressed—and the imprisonment or murder of those simply trying to provide humanitarian assistance? How else is it possible to express the illegal and arbitrary arrests, imprisonments, beating, and killing of individuals, their cold bodies returned to loved ones with crude lacerations roughly sewn up, as if their internal organs had been abruptly seized? What else can be said when land mines are carefully planted in people's homes, fields, places of faith, and schools, quietly awaiting their return from displacement?

Whether sampling through social media, the news, or personal conversation, it is clear that there is a deep pain felt across Myanmar, an aching for true peace, relief, and restoration.

Desert River

It is easy to be overwhelmed by the bad news in Myanmar, but the contributors and editors of this book feel it is time to highlight something else that's happening in the midst of such evil and violence. At a time when every political, economic, and social

---

[15] "Criticized, Myanmar's Influential Monk Close to Coup Leader Breaks Silence on Killing Protesters," The Irrawaddy, March 5, 2021, https://www.irrawaddy.com/news/burma/criticized-myanmars-influential-monk-close-coup-leader-breaks-silence-killing-protesters.html.

system is failing, a rebelling hope remains. In the midst of the depression, trauma, and doubt—which is undeniably there—the authors of these stories give accounts of God-given desert rivers: spaces that support new growth, deep change, even healing. These spaces can be immediate and overwhelming with the incomprehensible overflow of provision, but they can also feel gradual, protracted, and at times even unremarkable—a slow but steady trickle that can go unnoticed. In all of these spaces, God is there, and he is working.

These rivers in the desert are the stories we want to share. We want to talk about how God is moving, how he is still doing, even when evil seems to overwhelm and overpower every aspect of life. The river's appearance and its advance in the midst of violence does not always conform to our intuitive notions of solutions, power, or retributive justice, but it changes things in enduring ways. We are convinced that something is happening—though quietly, even secretly. And though we are limited by what we presently see and understand, these glimpses of his river reveal the beauty he is creating from the world's brokenness. And that is worth celebrating.

"My family and I had to run away because of bomb explosions and gunfire in our neighborhood."

"Because my father is a government [employee] and participated in the strike, he had to run away from home and hide, and our family cannot live together."

"Many [people] have had to make bomb shelters at home."

"A friend called me who was in the middle of armed conflict. I could hear shooting in the background. He said he couldn't stop shaking."

"Drunk soldiers forced me to show them my belongings and threatened me with their guns when I was returning home from grocery shopping."

"They raided our street at night. I saw soldiers shooting into people's houses."

SILENCE

Lord, it is so desolate here. There is no shade. There is no water. The riverbed is dry. It is hot, unforgiving, oppressive. Though I walk for days, months, years—all I can see is endless, harsh, unabating terrain. It would have me believe you have forgotten. Or that you were never here in the first place.

I'm afraid, Lord. More than death, I'm afraid of hope. I'm afraid of a hope that will be left unanswered, unfulfilled. I'm afraid of a hope that will hurt. That I will wait for you here but you will never come. That the promises I clasp in my hands will dissolve into sand at my feet.

Please give me strength and encouragement. Please give me confidence in your character. Please give me a stubborn determination to see your goodness. Please remind me that you have not abandoned me. That I can trust you. That I am special to you. That you are coming—no, that you have already arrived.

In your patience and mercy, please sensitize me to your presence.

The desert river you have made, the new thing you are doing in this wasteland—please lead me to it. Please open my eyes and my mind to see it.

Lead me back, again and again.

And give me life.

—A. M.

SCORCHED

Adjective. To be burned, marked, or scarred by overwhelming heat.

> He led you through the vast and dreadful wilderness, that thirsty and waterless land, with its venomous snakes and scorpions. He brought you water out of hard rock.
>
> —Deuteronomy 8:15

"[Because] I grew up fleeing from fighting, I hate civil wars. When I first heard the news about the military coup, I thought that I [would] have to run away and starve again. I felt afraid thinking that I [would] have to suffer again."

—Myanmar national

"Boys from my neighbourhood were arrested by the military. They were beaten and taken at night."

—Myanmar national

RUNNING

Adjective. Moving at an increased rate; the flowing of water from its source to its destination as it overcomes obstacles in its course.

My name is Saw Say. I am a pastor in a village located in Southeast Myanmar. Most of our villagers believe in traditional spirits, and there are only a few Christians. The village where I serve is in an area with a very sensitive political situation, as it is under two administrations.[1] Our village has to move frequently because of fighting, and when this happens, usually the villagers leave temporarily until the fighting subsides. However, the fighting that began in 2022 has become even more frequent and intense than the armed clashes before. As a result, the villagers cannot work in the fields. They often have to run away to escape the violence and return later.

In July 2022, violent and intense fighting took place near our village. We heard the sounds of heavy weapons and gunfire, and bullets fell among our homes. The villagers didn't dare to stay there anymore, and everyone ran into the forest. The fighting happened daily, and we could not go back to the village. It was very difficult to stay in the forest, as it was the monsoon season. After a few days, there wasn't much food left. At that time, a father and son from the village decided to risk going back to get some provisions. Shortly after they left, we heard intense fighting happening again. That evening, we heard the news that the father and son were hit by heavy weapons, and one of them had died instantly. We were very shocked.

The next day, some church members and I decided to go back to the village to get some rice, as there was no food left to eat. Before we started on our way to the village, we prayed together and placed our journey in God's hands. Although we were very

---

1 *Both the military-influenced government administration and ethnic organization administration.*

scared, we felt we had to make this sacrifice for our family and church members.

We started our trip back to the village on a very rainy night. By the grace of God, we arrived at the village safely and collected the necessary provisions. After preparing the items, we rested for a while, as we were exhausted. While we rested, a bomb dropped near us. We took everything and ran back into the dark forest without any flashlights. By the grace of God, we returned safely to the place where our community was sheltering in the forest. God was with us on our trip.

We had to stay in the forest for over a month. Because it was the monsoon season, there were health problems, food problems, and bad living conditions, and we could not stand staying there anymore. We discussed and prayed together, asking God to open the way for us. Within a short period of time, we connected with some teachers associated with a church, and we had the opportunity to take refuge in a town in that area. When we arrived in the town, God provided for us with food and health assistance. Although our migration period was very long, God never left us. God is always with us. God is good to us.

> **RESPONDING WITH PRAYER:**
>
> 1. Please pray for wisdom, encouragement, provision, and protection for Myanmar nationals currently sheltering in the jungle.
>
> 2. Read over and reflect on Psalm 142, written while David was sheltering in a cave. Lift up the people of Myanmar as you pray through this Psalm.
>
> 3. Are there areas in your own life where you are currently experiencing lack or difficulty? Take some time to ask God to make you aware of the ways he is present and providing even in those situations.

QUENCH

Verb. To satisfy thirst; to refresh in a dry environment.

My name is Naw Pway, and I am forty-five years old. When I was thirteen years old, my entire village was bombed, and my family and I had to flee to another village. When I was twenty-five years old, I got married, and my husband and I had five sons together. We tried very hard to take care of our family, but things were difficult. My husband was not healthy and could not work a lot, which added to the challenges we faced. When my sons got older, they could not go to school because they also had to work to earn money for our family. When the COVID-19 pandemic reached Myanmar, our situation became even more difficult with the challenges that came with the pandemic. Then the military coup took place. Things continued to get worse for our family.

My sons and I had to walk two miles away from our village for work, which consisted of harvesting beans from the fields. When we went to work one day, we could hear gunshots from fighting nearby, but we knew we had to keep working to provide for our family. The gunshots didn't stop but got louder and closer to us. We knew they were coming from fighting that was taking place near our village. Still, we decided to keep working to fulfill our promise to the farm owner.

In the afternoon, two airplanes of a type we had only seen in the movies passed over us and dropped bombs on a village some distance away. We could see it very clearly. I knew that it was not a dream, and the noises shook me. We had to run away to safety, and my sons and I rushed back to our village to find my husband so we could all run away together.

When we got halfway to the village, we saw others running away, and they stopped us from going back to the village. We were told that the entire village had fled and that there had been arrests and beatings by the Myanmar military. I cried when I heard the news—I didn't know what to do. I was so worried about my husband, wondering if he was alone somewhere. There were many families separated from each other, just like us. At that time, I remembered God, and I knew that only he could save us. I prayed to God to protect my husband and reunite our family. That night we slept in the forest. Due to the dangerous situation, we could not go back and had to sleep there for three nights. We had run into the forest with only the clothes we were wearing, so we couldn't hold on for long.

We tried to find the best route back to the village. When we arrived, there was no one there, and I could not find my husband. I cried, thinking that he had been arrested. Before I could stop crying, artillery shelling hit my village. My sons dragged me away, and we fled again. We ran in fear to a river about eight miles away from the west side of the village. All that long way, I prayed that my family would have an opportunity to be reunited completely.

After crossing the river and arriving on the other side, we saw the rescue vehicles of a Christian association coming to pick us up. Other villagers hurried to get in the cars. We got into a car too because we didn't know where to run. When the car arrived at a church in another town, they gave us food and arranged a place for us to stay. I could not eat anything. I was worried about my ailing husband, and I just cried. I prayed constantly to God for my family to be reunited. There were tens of thousands of people in this area, but no one knew about my husband. Some said that my husband might have been arrested. I wept and did not eat for eight days.

One morning, a number of days after arriving at this new town, a teacher I knew came to me and said that she had seen my husband at a center. As soon as I heard the news, I said tearful prayers and gave thanks to God. He allowed my family to be reunited. I realized how God had prepared our family and provided for us. In the past, we worked very hard just to get enough food for one day, but now, after more than three months, even though we cannot work or do anything due to the current situation, God has provided the food we need. It is food prepared by God. Before this, we struggled to eat and could not devote time to God. Now, because God has prepared food to eat, we have time to give back to him. So I pray to God and read the Bible as much as I can. I participate in a fasting-and-prayer program at church. I feel calm in my mind. The scripture that gives me strength is Psalm 23. As the Lord is my shepherd, he has reunited his divided family of sheep. There is nothing God cannot do. Even though we struggled a lot in the village to put rice in the rice pot, God has prepared the rice pot to be full of rice during difficult times. God is so good.

> **RESPONDING WITH PRAYER:**
>
> 1. Please pray for Myanmar families who have been separated by the current conflict. Consider praying through Psalm 23 for these families.
>
> 2. Do you have any relationships in your life where you are experiencing emotional and/or physical distance? Take some time to pray about that.

PSALM 23

The Lord is my shepherd, I lack nothing.
He makes me lie down in green pastures,
he leads me beside quiet waters,
he refreshes my soul.
He guides me along the right paths
for his name's sake.
Even though I walk
through the darkest valley,
I will fear no evil,
for you are with me;
your rod and your staff,
they comfort me.
You prepare a table before me
in the presence of my enemies.
You anoint my head with oil;
my cup overflows.
Surely your goodness and love will follow me
all the days of my life,
and I will dwell in the house of the Lord
forever.

SHADE

Noun. A place of momentary relief from the sun; shelter from heat.

I am a pastor's wife, and my husband and I have a son. He plays happily around our tent in the daytime. I keep watch over him while I'm working. But when the sun sets, he is too afraid to go anywhere alone. Someone has to be with him. It is the same with us—when we experience darkness, trials, and troubles, we wish for our Savior God to be with us all the time.

To be frank, I am easily scared. We all know that fear is a big obstacle—not only for our future but also for our mental health. That is why whenever I feel fear, I overcome it with God's promises in Scripture.

In May 2021, when my son was five, we heard fighting and explosions for the first time in a decade in my town. Even though the country had been struggling through a second wave of COVID-19, we were more afraid of the fighting than the pandemic. We heard the sound of armed clashes again the next day. Some people in our community ran away from home while some remained, thinking the fighting would end soon. Although our family planned to stay and hide at home, my son was still a child and could not stay silent, which increased the risk of soldiers coming to find us. I thought we might need to run away, and I prepared an emergency bag in advance.

One day, when my husband returned back home after putting up a white flag[1] at the church compound—which gave notice that we were there and running out of food—I talked to him about running away. He planned everything for me, but he could not come with us. From the start, he had told me that he wouldn't be able to leave, so I already knew he wouldn't be coming, and I understood why. My husband's parents were over eighty years

---

[1] *White flags are typically used to signify areas of nonviolence in situations of conflict.*

old and had decided to stay in the village come what may, so he needed to care for them. He also had remaining church members in the village and did not want to abandon them. For me, I left behind my small shop at the market where I sold traditional outfits, clothes, and local goods. Later, I found that all of my merchandise and even the cabinet had been stolen.

As I needed to do things by myself, I prayed to God to give me strength, and I left the village with my son. First, we went by truck to a safe village near us, which had been set up by the churches. Afterward, we traveled on foot or by motorbike. We stayed in a rice field before accompanying a friend's family to another village. We were very worried during the whole journey. We recited Bible verses, prayed to God, sighed out of anxiety and frustration, and kept watch over our surroundings so that we would not encounter military soldiers.

All the residents of the villages we passed had already fled, and the road was quiet and eerie with no people. Because of our fear and worry, the road also seemed longer than normal. It wasn't until we arrived at our destination several hours later that we felt we could finally breathe. There were so many people gathered in this village. If you didn't know the reason we were here, it would have seemed that we had all come to celebrate something.

As we all were displaced, each of us prepared a place to stay. We were being hosted safely by another villager, but there were so many people that we were packed in tightly. We cooked some food and ate quickly and prepared to spend the night in the dark. Just when we had prepared our beds, we heard a big explosion outside of town and saw a huge fire in the distance. There was nothing we could do except pray. All of us displaced Christians there prayed together for those in the distance suffering from attack.

A fighter jet passed over us when we tried to sleep again, and we were all afraid and on edge—we almost ran away again. That night, the jet only passed over us; nothing more happened. God knew that I could not run away with my emergency bag and my child again. It would have been more difficult at night, and we would be moving from place to place with nowhere to sleep and nothing to eat. Even today, I praise God for protecting me so I didn't have to flee that night.

After one week, our remaining family members could not live in our old town anymore, and they came to the village that my son and I were temporarily residing in. Our whole family, including my husband and his parents, was able to reunite. After around two weeks, however, the security situation in that village became hazardous, and we all needed to move again. We moved to another village called "TDK." It was very cold there. However, my husband returned back to our home village, as he was not only a church pastor but also a general secretary in the missionary field. He needed to arrange, manage, and prepare emergency support for church members. Even though I needed my husband during that time, I knew he was serving God. I was able to be a good support to him by understanding the importance of what he was doing.

I experienced many difficulties during our time of displacement. My son was sick with diarrhea, chicken pox, and toothaches, and he would cry in the middle of the night because he missed his father. As the new village was very cold, it was also very hard for my father-in-law, who had had a stroke; for my mother-in-law, who had gout; and for me, as I had painful arthritis.

Because of the cold, we moved again to another village called "HLPK." This was an area where most of those who were displaced lived. The place had flat ground and a lot of sunlight, and it was a better place for my family and me. I was overjoyed that our family could reunite in that village.

But then we all began to feel what displaced people normally feel—after staying there for two months, we felt that we had already been living in other people's houses a long time, and we felt sorry for the villagers who had accepted us into their homes. Even though the community welcomed us, we felt sorry for being a burden. That's why, when the fighting stopped temporarily, we returned to our original town. Although it was still not safe, we felt more comfortable in our own homes. Of course, we prepared our go-bags to be ready if we needed to leave again. Sadly, on the way back to our hometown my mother-in-law's health became worse, and she passed away. We had funeral services immediately.

On September 7, 2022, a day now known as D-Day [when the National Unity Government (NUG) officially encouraged people to work together against the military], fighting started in the township police station. We were stuck in the middle of the fighting zone, as our home was near where the violence was taking place. Bullets and other weapons were close enough to reach us at any time. By the grace of God, we were able to keep safe. We ran away again the next day.

As we were displaced again, we returned to a village near our hometown and built a tent in a field just outside the village. Other villagers began to live there, too. It was just fifteen or twenty minutes away from our hometown, one of the main fighting hotspots. We lived together with the noises of gunfire and artillery. We could clearly see fighter jets dropping bombs. One time we saw two big lights in the sky that we thought were floating lanterns at first, but after they exploded right above us, we realized we had seen a rocket launcher.

We prepared food for emergencies. At first, my family members would send some rations from far away if the roads were open. Later, the roads closed, and my family members became displaced themselves, and they could not send us food anymore.

It has been a year since we began living here. As we do not know when this war will end, we raise animals and do some gardening in the village. Being a servant of God has taught me to take care of others. Our village is not included on the donation list for churches or NGOs (nongovernmental organizations),[2] since we

---

2 *Nongovernmental organizations (NGOs) and international nongovernmental organizations (INGOs) are nonprofit organizations that do social or humanitarian work around the world.*

43

are not within the donors' target area. Also, because we live on our own land, we are not included on the displaced persons list. That is why we have worked so hard. Working not only relieves our stress but also makes us happy. We grow some plants and raise chickens, ducks, and fish. We have a chance to share our farm products with others. Even though we still hear the sounds of gunfire and explosions, we keep doing what we can, especially farming rice, peanuts, sesame, and sunflowers. By the grace of God, we have never starved, not even for one day.

The challenge our family faces during this time is worrying for my husband who, as a missionary, needs to travel often, and so is at risk of encountering unexpected fighting. I also worry about how we will run if any emergency happens.

Once I asked my husband, "Can't you just stay back this one time?" He was taking a trip to support communities and traveling to a place other pastors could rarely reach, both because of its location and because of the fighting. He answered me by saying that if the assigned person does not want to go, he has to go because he is the leader. He said, "Being a leader means doing what others do not want to do. If no one wants to go, we cannot finish our work." After hearing his answer, I could only understand his reasons and agree to let him go.

Whenever he travels, those of us who remain hold on even more tightly to God. I survive these times by having faith in God that as my husband is working for God and his kingdom, God will take care of his family. I pray for God's protection wherever my husband goes. God really protects us and is with us always, and I myself have expanded my circle of trust and spiritual maturity through these difficulties.

Since first being displaced, we have been very thankful to God when we are able to sleep well at night. Gun and artillery fire can be shot at any place at any time, so the conditions are not safe. Sometimes live ammunition lands near our village; other times, it passes above us. These occasions seem normal for us now. We are okay only because we put our lives in God's hands. Nothing is possible without God. We have felt that we are stronger in Christ the more difficulties we experience. Only with God's protection are we safe.

Whatever happens, I know that during this displaced time I have actively experienced the fact that God always takes care of us and is with us all the time.

I would like to end with 1 Peter 5:7: "Cast all your anxiety on him because he cares for you."

RESPONDING WITH PRAYER:

1. Please pray for strength and endurance for Myanmar families who are repeatedly displaced because of the conflict. Pray for family members who need to travel for work in unsafe situations and for the relatives who wait for them back home.

2. The author feels that the more she experiences difficulties in her life, the stronger she is in Christ. What's your perspective on that in your own life with the challenges you've experienced (or are currently experiencing)? Take some time to talk with God about that.

"When I had to flee suddenly from my home, [I felt] so disappointed and dispirited. It was so comfortable and convenient at my own house, with my job, income, and family. The feeling of leaving home is like throwing away all the important things and wandering off to an unknown place. That place was a new environment; everything was new for me, and no friends were there. After living there for about one month, I heard that there might be fighting in this area, so we dug big holes behind the house to hide. I was so worried when I heard the news, but nothing happened at that time. After about three or four months, I again heard news that there was going to be a war. This time the war was real, and I had to flee from that place.

When we heard that the Myanmar soldiers were coming, we ran into the forest at night through a harvested cornfield. We could not see anything very well, so my legs were stabbed with corn stalks, but at that time I could not care. When I hid in the forest and sat under a tree, a lot of insects bit my whole body, but I didn't dare move or make noise. I had to stay just like that. It was just one night. [For] people who [are] in the forests for a long time due to wars, I cannot imagine how difficult it [is] for them.

I was very scared, but God is good. As he is a God who works with time, he saved me from the war ahead of time. God is good all the time."

—Myanmar national

"It is stressful for me to live apart from my family during these times. I have been constantly worrying for them and [it] is the same for them. In these days, due to fighting and military checkpoints on the way to my home, I [can't] travel freely and easily which frustrates me a lot."

—Myanmar national

OASIS

Noun. A place of life and refuge in the midst of an otherwise lifeless or life-threatening area; a place where water is found in the desert.

I would like to tell you about how God has moved in my life recently. After the military coup in Myanmar, everyone felt distressed and hopeless. I, too, felt that there was no hope for my future, but then I felt God tell me to find hope in him. If God didn't help us, there was no one who could. We can only hope in God.

In a village near the Myanmar-Thai border, I served in a ministry as an assistant sewing teacher. After the military coup, the situation in the village became very tense. Fighting broke out between the Myanmar military and an ethnic armed organization in our neighborhood. While the tension there was escalating, myself, six students, and another teacher became trapped between the two armies for about two hours. We could hear gunfire as the Myanmar military attacked. The gunshots were so clear, so close, and so loud. My students were extremely scared, in shock, and crying. I tried to comfort them and help them keep quiet to avoid being shot by the Myanmar military; I knew the military's reputation of killing anyone they could find, whether armed soldier or unarmed civilian.

In the midst of the shooting, cries, and chaos, I remembered 1 Peter 5:7, which says, "Cast all your anxiety on him because he cares for you." In that moment, I gave all of my worries to God.

By the grace of God, the ethnic armed organization soldiers came and helped us to escape the gunfire. We immediately moved to the next village and stayed for one night, then moved to another village for another night, and so on. Eventually we came to the Myanmar-Thai border. We stayed at a border camp for eight days, but soon the Myanmar military began attacking again, shooting rocket-propelled grenades (RPGs) near the camp. So many people were confused and panicked in the chaos, and many tried to cross the river to safety on the Thai side.

However, not all were allowed to cross, and our group was split—while two of my students made it to the other side, four other students and myself were stranded on the Myanmar side. Day and night, Thai soldiers patrolled the border with their automatic weapons loaded and with authorization to shoot anyone crossing the border without permission. This made finding safety on the Thai side a very dangerous endeavor.

Again I prayed to God, asking him to give us safe passage across the Thai border. The camp was still unsafe and prone to attacks from the Myanmar military. We were effectively trapped between armed conflicts and a closed border. I only had the equivalent of five dollars in my hand and no resources or connections to help me cross the border. Again, by the grace of God, I was able to meet with someone willing to assist us across even though it was very dangerous.

Even though we had to hide in cornfields at first to avoid being detected, we were eventually able to cross safely and receive help. Ever since I arrived on the Thai side of the border I have been participating in ministry and sharing the gospel with people here. I never thought I would be involved in God's work full time, but God is using me now. I am now serving as a full-time minister at a church. I also help take care of the children who have escaped from the war, and God uses me to support them spiritually as well. As it says in Romans 12:21, "Do not be overcome by evil, but overcome evil with good." Let us continue to work for God's glory and remember God's goodness and faithfulness even in this difficult situation.

God's plan is better than our plan. God's plan is the best for us and for the people of Myanmar. Let us continue to pray and find hope in him.

RESPONDING WITH PRAYER:

1. Please pray that Myanmar nationals running away from violence will be able to find safety, including those needing to enter other countries.

2. Have you ever felt trapped in a situation? Spend time reflecting on how God may have been working in that time and thank him for the ways he provided.

CHANNEL

Noun. A natural or created path that directs the flow of water.

I would like to share one of the many times God has done unbelievable things in my life. I grew up in a remote rural town in the mountains. My parents had a clothing store and grocery shop in our town. After the 2021 military coup, fighting started, and we dared not live in our town anymore; we had to run away. My parents and brothers ran away to a different village, and I moved to the town where my husband works. When we ran away, we were all in a hurry, and we left behind everything we had. After I was displaced to this new area, I thought about going back and taking things we had left in our shop. I had recently bought a brand-new motorbike, and I really wanted to go back to get it.

However, my husband disagreed with the idea of going back home, as it was not safe. One day when he was at work, I snuck back to our home without telling him. I went with a car that could only fit three suitcases—but God is very good. I met the drivers of two light trucks just outside of town. Even though they didn't want to come back with me, I asked them to help me, as I really needed their assistance. As I knew soldiers were guarding the road the whole way, I contacted one officer that I knew to open the road for us. I explained that I needed to make a living, so I had to retrieve things that we had left there. He agreed to open the road, and we arrived safely. We packed urgently and put everything that we could in the trucks.

On the way back, I drove my motorbike, and the light trucks followed. While we were driving, soldiers who were stationed on the mountain above threw a bomb at us. By God's grace, the bomb narrowly missed us, falling into the slope in front of us. After the bomb, the soldiers shot their guns at us continuously. We all were very afraid, and I abandoned my motorbike and jumped into the ditch. I recited all the Bible verses I remembered and prayed to

God. The others I was with also hid under their vehicles from the gunfire.

When the shooting paused, we went back the way we came and took a detour into ethnic resistance territory, which was a very far and long route compared to the original one. Per the ethnic army's advice, we waited until all the shooting had finished and then returned back to town. We arrived safely by the grace of God. Amazingly, there was no damage to anything, and everything that we brought from home was in good condition.

Purely by his grace, God not only prepared the way but also sent the trucks we needed for transportation. I thank God for his protection and guidance. During the shooting, I thought I would die. There was nothing I could have done if God had not protected me.

RESPONDING WITH PRAYER:

1. Please pray for Myanmar families who have lost access to their jobs. Pray for safe work opportunities.
2. How have you seen God redeem a situation in your life? Take time to thank him for his mercy.

SWELL

*Noun. The amassing of a body of water such that
it moves forward with force.
Verb. To surge.*

My name is Saw Keh Say. Even though I grew up in difficult times, I became grateful for them after learning more about God's plan. When I was a young child, I had to run away from war in my village. As I was so young, I cried and got into trouble for being too loud. Soldiers were coming from another village to our village. They would be crossing near where we hid. It was not safe for the other villagers to travel with us for fear that I might cry and give away our hiding spot, so I was sent to an orphanage. I was only three or four years old. For ten years, I stayed at the orphanage and attended school there. When I was fourteen, I was able to live with my family in a refugee camp in Thailand, and I continued my studies at a school there.

For a period of time, there were fewer wars in Myanmar, and I could see the country developing. I decided to return to Myanmar for work and to try to improve my life. I was doing fine before the military staged a coup in February 2021—I even planned to ask my mother and sister, who were still in a refugee camp in Thailand, to join me. However, all of my plans were ruined after the coup. I had to migrate due to the lack of work and because of the insecurity and instability the coup created.

The security situation in Myanmar challenged me. The army only abides by the law when it is convenient for them; otherwise, there are no ethical standards—they just do what they want. This means it can be very dangerous to cross paths with the military. Due to increased violence and lack of trust in the security forces, communities organized their own community-watch groups to stand guard each night and protect their neighborhoods. This was dangerous. The military enforced a curfew, and soldiers would often come around and shoot people who were disobeying. On the other hand, if we refused to help stand guard, the community would accuse us of supporting the military.

I hoped that the political crisis would somehow be resolved soon. I didn't want to leave Myanmar in case things got better, so I moved to safer places, which were controlled by one of the ethnic armed groups. The last village I lived in faced a huge armed attack. Even now, there are still attacks happening in that place. By the grace of God, one Christian organization helped our group. We were able to escape just in time and move to another place. As soon as we left the village, the fighting started.

Everyone advised us to move to Thailand, but I wanted to stay in Myanmar—we knew that it would cost more if we moved to Thailand, and we didn't have enough money. At that time, God spoke to me through the Bible with Matthew 14:29–30 [when Jesus calls Peter to walk to him on the water]. Just as God called Peter into strong winds and impossibility, he was calling me. I worried because the situation was dire, but God told me, "Even Peter, who was an expert fisherman and expert in the water, could drown. Don't try and rely on yourself like Peter, who thought he was an expert in water. Just rely on me." What I finally understood was that if God called me, he would take responsibility for everything. If he called me, he would provide for me. Even if a situation seems hopeless, he wants us to rely on him. When I choose to walk with faith, God is able to lead me to the blessings he's prepared for me. Even though I was concerned about the likelihood of financial difficulties and police arrests in Thailand, God changed my thoughts, opinions, and heart.

It was only by the grace of God that I was able to celebrate my wedding in Thailand. I saw the increase in provision for our wedding ceremony according to God's promise. When we were planning our wedding, we only had 30,000 baht (851 USD) in our hands. We tried to plan the wedding with 40,000 baht. We asked to borrow some money from our friends, but it didn't work out even though we were willing to borrow with interest. We were really worried for our wedding, but we decided to just move forward with the money we had in our hands.

Our wedding was beautiful. Afterward, my wife and I held each other's hands to worship, and we thanked God. When we calculated our wedding expenses, we realized the wedding had cost around 70,000 baht, but we hadn't gone into debt. Wow! We were really surprised! We asked each other, "Where did that money come from?" The answer was God's plan. God made our wedding beautiful and wonderful with all that we had. God provided what we needed in unexpected ways and from unexpected people.

We realized that God's plan was truly the best for us. If we had borrowed money with interest, we would have had debt, and we would have had to worry about paying it back. God didn't want us to live in debt. He wants us to experience his beautiful plan and his promises. We might forget what we ask and what his promises are, but he never will. God is good all the time.

I praise the name of God, who made a covenant with me and always wants to bless me. May the name of God be glorified. God's glory is evident in my life whenever I face difficulties. I pray for those who have not yet experienced his works, that they would see God's provision in their lives. Myanmar is currently facing poverty and war. In the midst of that, I believe that the people of Myanmar will experience God's new works, just as I have experienced them.

RESPONDING WITH PRAYER:

1. Please pray for Myanmar children impacted by armed conflict.

2. Do you remember a time in your life where God provided for you in an unexpected way? Take some time to thank him for his faithful provision.

"It deeply moved me when a friend of mine, who is part of the People's Defence Force, shared a powerful account of how God moved to protect his people. In the face of escalating violence, the military resorted to using air strikes, shifting their tactics to target innocent civilians. He said, 'We witnessed air strikes demolishing some villages in the distance from our camp, and we feared that all our people would be killed. We felt helpless, and there was nothing we could do. At that moment, I saw our chief commander opening the Bible and reading it on his knee at the corner of our shelter. He wept, and we all joined him in prayer in the middle of the incident. God never abandoned us. He protected every single one of our people that day.'"

—Myanmar national

FOR DEEPER REFLECTION:

1. Reflect on Isaiah 43:19. What is a "desert river"? How have you seen this theme play out in the stories so far? How have you seen this theme in your own life?

2. How do you feel when reading these stories of Myanmar nationals thanking God in extremely challenging circumstances? What thoughts and emotions does this trigger in you?

PARCHED

Adjective. The condition of the body's crying out as a result of prolonged dryness; a somatic sensation of desperation.

> You, God, are my God, earnestly I seek you; I thirst for you, my whole being longs for you, in a dry and parched land where there is no water.
>
> —Psalm 63:1

"When the third wave of COVID-19 hit Myanmar, there were many seriously ill COVID-19 patients. Very few hospitals were accepting those patients, so the people had no choice but to take care of their loved ones at home. With the military threat happening around [us], not enough health care workers, lack of health care knowledge, and shortage of oxygen, it made the daily death rate [skyrocket] in August. People were lining up to fill up their oxygen tanks."

—Myanmar national

"Starting [in] February, I was very worried for my family and also for myself. This [led] to me having a difficult time with exhaustion and also depression."

—Myanmar national

FISH

*Noun. A creature that flourishes in bodies of water;
a source of sustenance.
Verb. Attempting to draw out something that will bring satisfaction.*

I was sitting in the dark in a small restaurant, and I was angry. I was feeling the itching pangs of addiction, but my friend—a drug dealer—could not meet with me. Little did I know that this night God would change the direction of my whole life. Forever.

I grew up very poor. I never had new clothes or sandals, and often my trousers were in disrepair. My parents came from different backgrounds—my father was Buddhist and my mother Christian. In order for my father to marry my mother, he got baptized—but he didn't know anything about Jesus. I grew up knowing more about Buddha than Jesus, as my grandfather lived with us and talked about Buddha a lot. We went to many pagodas, and I was a student at the temple.

My father was an alcoholic and constantly drank. The Christian community discriminated against our family and blamed us for this. I sold flowers in the local wet market[1] to try to earn money. Sometimes I would stay and serve fruit to the Buddhist monks who would walk through asking for alms. I remember thinking that one day I wanted to help others like me.

Eventually my parents separated. When I was thirteen years old, I moved to the city of Yangon to live with my father while my mother and elder sister lived together elsewhere. By this time, he had overcome his issues with drinking because, he said, he had heard the voice of God. He had accepted Jesus, and he brought me to a Christian summer camp. At that summer camp, I also accepted Jesus—and even got baptized—but soon thereafter, I fell into sin.

---
1 *A public marketplace selling fresh produce and meat.*

When I was fifteen years old, I started using drugs.

I didn't need to be tempted to start using drugs—no one convinced me to or led me astray. In fact, I was usually the one leading others astray. I didn't know how to deal with my emotions and childhood trauma. I wanted to fight, do drugs, drink alcohol, and do things that people didn't want me to do. My drugs of choice were *yama* (methamphetamines mixed with caffeine) and ice (crystal methamphetamine).

Typically, after using, I would feel that the drugs weren't good enough—like they weren't enough for my soul. So, I'd play guitar. I came back to this one song time and time again—"I Want to Be Close with God." While the drugs didn't give me peace, playing guitar and worshiping God did. In fact, there were two times when I was singing that I heard angels' voices. I thought it was the drugs, but it had never happened before.

And then, at thirty-two years old, I found myself in the dark, in a small restaurant. The electricity had been cut, and the whole ward was experiencing a power outage. The shop used small candles in an attempt to provide customers enough light to see their food. I had arranged to meet with the friend who supplied my drugs, but he hadn't shown up. I was a regular customer of his, so it made me angry. I myself sold rice, so I understood the principles of customer service, and I found his especially lacking. I really wanted to use, so I was getting very frustrated.

Then I heard a voice saying, "Look at the wrong you are doing."

I looked around, wondering who was talking to me. The darkness surrounded me. I could barely see anything. I thought I was hallucinating, but I hadn't used any drugs yet.

Again, the voice said, "Look at your life."

The darkness from the power outage—it was all around me. It echoed the darkness in my life. I had a broken family, debt issues, and a lot of emotional problems and trauma resulting from years of neglect and rejection. Everyone had left me. My life felt like it was falling apart, like it was broken.

The voice continued, "As with this darkness now, why is your life so dark? Why is it falling apart?"

He answered for me, "Because you are not staying with me."

I am not afraid of anything. I am not afraid of the mafia, or fights, or death. When I was growing up, I was the one to chase those kinds of situations. But in that moment, I understood what it meant to fear God. I repented, directly and immediately. I knew I was broken inside.

I asked him, "God, how do I overcome my addiction? How can I stop living the life of a drug addict?" and he said, "You cannot overcome it by yourself. But you can overcome it through my power, grace, and love."

I prayed to God to give me strength. I told him I didn't want to use drugs or be led by my emotions. I told him, "I give my life to You."

That night, by the grace of God, I was healed from my drug addiction. I knew I was changed—and the days that followed proved it. I didn't need to undergo treatment from any doctor, or go to a counselor, or get help for withdrawal symptoms. By human standards I knew this would have been impossible, given the significant quantity I had been ingesting and the consistency with which I had been doing drugs.

After that night, instead of being hungry for drugs, I hungered for God. I had never read the Bible or prayed to God—I know that it was only by the power of the Holy Spirit that I hungered for him. I joined a church community and participated in many opportunities for evangelism. I shared my testimony, served in church, and chose the way of Jesus. By the grace of God, I have been able to serve those who, like me, haven't had a lot of opportunities for education or successful futures and can't afford any new clothes.

I have not touched drugs since that fateful night six years ago. In the time since, I have seen many miracles from God. I have been able to help internally displaced people (IDPs)[2] and refugees in our country's current situation, and I helped start a church on the Thai border. By the grace of God, it has grown from 4 people to 150 people. Our members may have lost family in Myanmar, but they have been able to join a kingdom family here.

Before, I would be triggered to use drugs when I felt emotional or overwhelmed. I would be a slave to my emotions and then try to ease them with drugs. Now, when those times come, I have a strange craving: I only want to eat fish. If I become angry, I want to eat fish. If painful memories are triggered, I want to eat fish. In the midst of doubt and loss, I want to eat fish. My yearning for drugs has been replaced with a craving for fish. It may sound strange, but I know where it comes from. Each time I have a craving to eat fish, it reminds me of Jesus cooking fish on the shore for his disciples—his disciples who were grieving, lost, broken, and desperate for him.

So, come. He has the food we need. Come to him, and eat fish.

---

2 *Internally Displaced People (IDPs) are people who are forced to flee their homes for a different part of the same country. Refugees, on the other hand, are people who are forced to flee their home country and escape to another country for refuge.*

RESPONDING WITH PRAYER:

1. Please pray for those struggling with addiction in Myanmar. Pray for breakthrough and access to support services.

2. Is there anything in your life that holds undue power or influence over you? Take some time to intentionally invite the Holy Spirit into that part of your life.

CLEAR

Adjective. A degree of clarity provided by clean water; without obstruction.

Before sharing my testimony, I would like to recite one Bible verse, Psalm 121:8: "The Lord will watch over your coming and going both now and forevermore."

My name is John. I would like to praise God first, who has let me live to this day. I am only alive today by the grace of God. God rescued me from the hand of death in 2014.

I got my first job in December 2013, working on a cargo ship at sea. I experienced many difficulties there. The working conditions were totally different from those on land. I was homesick. I could not sleep well on the ship, and I was dizzy because of the waves. There were language barriers and expectation gaps. I cried every day, and I always prayed that my work would go smoothly. After a few months of working, everything started to go well for me. As things got easier, I started to forget about God. I also started to use alcohol as a coping mechanism. When the ship came to dock and unloaded at the harbor, I started to behave in ways that displeased God.

I felt the impact of the work of Satan in October 2014. After my shift at work, I played table tennis with friends, had bread and fried fish paste, and then slept. At around three o'clock in the morning, I woke up with a stomachache. When I resumed my shift, my stomach pain became severe. There were still two days left until we would be able to dock at the harbor in Singapore. I had to endure the stomach pain while waiting to dock. Finally we arrived, but there was no ambulance, and I had to walk the jetty. The pain was so unbearable that I felt I was going to die.

When I checked in at the clinic, my situation was so serious that they had to immediately transfer me to a hospital. Following the check-up process, the hospital informed me that I had a fifty-fifty chance of survival. I didn't have a normal stomachache but a perforated appendix. My appendix had already burst, and all the toxins had seeped out, almost reaching my heart. A first surgery was completed, but it was not successful—toxins were still left in my stomach. A second surgery was attempted, but toxins were still left near my kidney, and so a third was commissioned. In total, I had three major operations and two minor operations to pump out the toxins.

After all of these operations, the doctors said, "You are a lucky man." They told me that death is possible if no action is taken within six hours of an appendix rupture. However, in my case I lived two days on the ship after my appendix burst. I was at the hospital for two months. Whenever I think about this, I feel God's mercy on me. This is a miracle. When I reflect on my experience, I have a deeper understanding of the fragility of human life and God's power to leave us on earth for his glory. As it says in Proverbs 3:12: "The Lord disciplines those he loves, as a father the son he delights in."

Finally, I would like to thank God again for letting me live to this day. I would like to encourage everyone to live as a child of God, in his will. No matter how many times the doctors tell me I am lucky, I know that without God, I would have died a very long time ago. I would like to end my testimony with Matthew 10:29: "Are not two sparrows sold for a penny? Yet not one of them will fall to the ground outside your Father's care."

May God bless you all.

> **RESPONDING WITH PRAYER:**
> 1. Please pray for Myanmar sailors who work long hours away from home and worry for the safety of their families in the current conflict.
> 2. Can you remember a time when you could clearly see God's grace and protection in a situation that seemed hopeless? Take time to remember, reflect, and thank God.

IMMERSE

Verb. To be wholly submerged in water; to be completely surrounded.

I am a teacher and a mother of two young boys. I would like to share how amazing our God is. He can do unbelievable things, and he has done unimaginable things in my life, things people said were impossible. It is proof that God can do what men can't do.

The year 2020 was a rough year for my family, even though it is more difficult now since the military coup. At the end of 2020, my whole family became infected with COVID-19. I was seven months pregnant at the time and had a two-year-old son. My obstetrician-gynecologist found that my placenta had been partially destroyed, and she was worried that something might happen to my child because of this complication. The child receives nutrients from the mother through the placenta, and since mine was damaged, all of the baby's functions started to slow down, and it could not grow normally. She referred me to the doctor from the children's ward and told me to prepare in case of a premature birth.

During that time, the coup happened. The public could not accept it and started to protest peacefully. Things got worse, and students and government staff from different sectors (teachers, doctors, nurses, lawyers, administrators, etc.) started a civil disobedience movement (CDM) to resist military administration. Hospitals could not operate anymore, as there were no doctors or nurses. The doctor I was referred to told me there were only military hospitals left, so I should plan to give birth there.

One doctor advised me to do a C-section, offering to schedule an appointment and handle the process. She reasoned that the child would not be able to handle the stress of being pushed out naturally. My first son had been born naturally, and I had recovered quickly afterward. I didn't want to have a C-section this time because I knew I would need proper rest afterward to let the incision heal. Due to my family's situation, I knew that wouldn't be possible, as no one could help me with both children. In addition, the cost of a C-section, including the surgery and subsequent hospital stay, was incredibly high, at least ten times higher than a natural birth at the hospital.

However, I was already seven months along. The doctor wanted me to choose a surgery date in March, but my due date was in April. Before deciding on the operation date, I went to another doctor for a second opinion, and he told me that I could have a natural birth. I was so happy. However, the hospital was quite far from my home. I prayed to God, telling him that he knew everything about my situation. I asked him to help me have a natural birth—or if not, to allow me to do a C-section at a hospital where the cost was relatively less than the others.

On Friday, February 26, 2021, I felt contractions the whole day. I had almost completed my seventh month of pregnancy, but there were still eight weeks left until my official due date. As there was still time left, I did not think I should be feeling labor pains yet. I suffered from the pain all day and night. I called a midwife I knew and asked her to come and check me. She confirmed that my cervix had not dilated enough yet. However, the pain was severe, so she suggested we go to the hospital. We prepared to go. My family members went downstairs, but I could not sit or stand and could not move at all. I felt that I needed to use the toilet. When I tried to go, I could not stand properly, and the pain intensified, so I pushed hard. My water broke.

When my first child was born, my water didn't break, and the doctors broke it manually, so I didn't have any experience to compare this to. This time, I felt something break, and water and some blood came out of me. When I saw blood, I was so frightened, as I knew the child was going to come out. My mind pleaded, "God help me and help the child!"—and I cried aloud too because of the intense pain. I pushed hard, and the child's head came out. I was scared. Before I was sure it was the child's head, I heard a cry. Shocked, I called my sister, and she came and held the baby's head. I was standing, giving birth in the bathroom. I kept pushing while my sister held the baby's head, and I praised God when his whole body came out. It was a terrifying time. If the umbilical cord had been wrapped around the child or we needed medical support, both he and I would have been in danger. By God's grace, I was able to give birth without complications.

With my first child, everything was handled by medical staff at the hospital, and I didn't need to worry about anything. For my second child, it was such a shocking experience as it was an emergency birth, and none of my family members were knowledgeable about labor and delivery. No one knew when or how to cut the umbilical cord for the child, so we delayed in cutting it. Even though I had researched it earlier, I forgot everything in the moment. The birth stunned everyone, and no one knew what to do.

Because my son was born prematurely, he had to be hospitalized. We experienced many critical moments after his birth, during the process of going to the hospital and getting him medical support. Myanmar's political situation made going to the hospital dangerous, but we arrived in time, and God sent us a good physician. As the baby had jaundice, he was given phototherapy as well as daily and nightly blood tests due to low sugar levels. His situation improved after a week. I named him Shaphan because he was wise and did not give up even though he was small.

Due to his unusual birth, his development was delayed, but today he is doing well in physiotherapy. Because of God's power and grace, he survived and is improving even though children can die if they are born at seven months. All the pediatricians were surprised because of this amazing occurrence. We really felt God's love and mercy.

I praise God for answering my prayer. I didn't want a C-section, and he let me have a natural birth. The doctor told me it was impossible to have a natural birth—much less a birth at home—and God let Shaphan come out smoothly. The doctor asked me to choose a date to do the C-section, but I gave birth according to God's time.

Our human ability is limited, but God is limitless. I would like to encourage you to have faith in God's ability. This testimony is also a reminder for me to look back on whenever I doubt God in this difficult time. May God bless us all abundantly.

RESPONDING WITH PRAYER:

1. Please pray for pregnant women and mothers in Myanmar. Pray for access to the medical assistance and resources they need as well as for protection for them and their children against the harmful impacts of trauma.

2. Reflect on a time when something important didn't go according to plan. Think about how God showed up in that situation and take time to thank him for that.

"Running away from the conflict and being displaced in the jungle brought so many challenges to each of us both physically and mentally. Physically we had no shelter. We did not have enough food, water, or medical supplies to survive in the jungle. Moreover, we had to sleep on muddy ground because it was the rainy season, and the danger of mosquitoes[1] was significant. Among the internally displaced people, the vulnerable groups such as elderly people, children, and pregnant women faced more challenges due to their physical weakness. They got sick more easily than the other groups but could not receive any treatment. Mentally, we felt insecurity. We lost our hope, since we had left our livelihoods and all our activities behind. We felt like our lives were already dead because most of our houses were destroyed by the artillery, and some of our relatives were killed during the conflict."

—Myanmar national

---

[1] *Mosquito-borne diseases in Myanmar include malaria, dengue, Zika, and chikungunya, and the risk of transmission is especially high during the monsoon season.*

REFRESH

Verb. To relieve or satisfy after a period of thirst.

I live with my mother, my husband, and my baby boy in the city. I run a stationery shop and provide photocopying and typing services. I have felt much of God's goodness in my life. I would like to share a situation that was surprising and seemed hopeless. On June 20, 2018, my husband, who had high blood pressure, suffered a stroke. One cerebral blood vessel burst, and three were blocked. At that time, I was eight months pregnant. The doctor said that if surgery was needed, it had to be done immediately. He said the chance of the surgery being successful was only 50 percent. I also knew that if the operation was unsuccessful, my husband could die. If my husband died, the baby in my womb would not have a father. That would break me.

I prayed to God because only he could redeem this situation. All our loving friends and family members also prayed for us. In the evening, the doctor came to discuss the situation with us. He said, "It is fine if you don't want to operate. Half of his body is damaged from the stroke. But he will improve if he takes medicine regularly and exercises regularly. It is not easy to get back to normal. However, if you compare it to a failed surgery and death, it is still better."

I was really happy and gave thanks to God that my husband didn't have to risk surgery. After one week, he was discharged from the hospital and returned home well. So far, my husband has not been able to move his leg and arm well on one side. Even though I feel a little more tired by caring for my husband and my son and working for my family's livelihood, God has given me the strength to endure.

In conclusion, I give thanks and glory to God for being able to witness that God's timing is best and his plan is never wrong. To face this challenging situation, God's promise of "being perfect in weakness" (2 Corinthians 12:9) gave me strength, and I can stand and survive today because of it. Never give up on God's promises. Walk with God. Admit his will. I share the goodness of God while praising him and believing that he will do the best thing in his time. He makes all things beautiful.

> **RESPONDING WITH PRAYER:**
>
> 1. Please pray for people in Myanmar who have had to become caretakers in addition to their other responsibilities. Pray for wisdom, provision, and opportunities for rest.
> 2. Consider all the different decisions you are currently faced with. Take time to ask God for wisdom and discernment.

REVIVE

Verb. To give life to; to be brought back from the brink of despair; to recover life through the provision of water.

My name is Maung Win Soe. Firstly, I would like to praise God, who is good all the time. I would like to share my personal testimony about the dislocation of my hip joint when I was working on a ship as a crew member. During a storm, water seeped into the food storeroom, and we had to quickly move the food. I slipped and fell from the stairs, landing on my hip. I felt mild, sharp pain in my waist the next day. But as it was not serious, I worked well until my contract ended.

After I returned home, one morning around 2 a.m., my grandma, who had had a stroke, called me to help her to go to the toilet. As I was very sleepy, I did not realize my body position, and as I lifted my grandma from the bed, I felt a very sharp pain in my waist. I strained myself in order to not drop her, and I put her back down on the bed. After that, I couldn't stand up, and I crawled back to my bed. I could not sleep and had to bend my knees the whole night to try to relieve the pain.

In the morning, my waist hurt very much, and I was not able to get up. I went to an orthopedic hospital with my mother for a medical checkup. The results showed that I needed to have surgery. I was afraid and depressed. I whispered to God, "God, I don't want to do the surgery. I don't have money. If any mistake happens during surgery, my lower body won't be able to move, and I won't be able to walk. Help me. I totally trust in what you can do."

There are two verses that make me feel calm, and I declared them every day, reciting, "I can do all things through him who gives me strength" (Philippians 4:13) and "By his wounds I have been healed" (1 Peter 2:24). I received God's mercy, and he gave me a gift. Instead of surgery, I received acupuncture seven times, and I used a Korean massage bed[1] two times per day for four consecutive months. I was able to walk again after this treatment. Encouraged by these results, my cousin bought me an expensive Korean massage bed that I could use daily. Because my back got better, I was able to attend Sunday church programs regularly, and there I met the girl who would later become my wife. I thank God for his healing and provision in my life.

---

[1] *A bed that uses heat therapy to massage the back.*

> **RESPONDING WITH PRAYER:**
>
> 1. Read Psalm 66. Please thank God for the healing he has provided and continues to provide to people in Myanmar.
>
> 2. Take time to identify powerful verses you can draw strength from in your current situation. Meditate on those verses and pray into them.

COVERED

Verb. To be enveloped, as with water over a riverbed; to be protected.

Praise the Lord as he is good and his mercy endures forever. Hallelujah!

I would like to thank God for giving me a chance to share his goodness in my life with this message. May he be glorified. As humans, we all have our own situations and problems. I am no different.

I run a grocery store in a community with my husband. We live with his family, and I care for my mother-in-law. Before this, I worked at a restaurant in Japan for some years and experienced many challenges. Even though I put my heart into my work, there were still rules and regulations and problems. I was always stressed. My coworkers would complain about me and blame me for things that went wrong because they disliked me. I started to feel that I was useless and worthless and that it would be better if I were dead.

I passed my days with these negative thoughts. One day I reflected on the words "blame" and "sin"—blame/sin from other people and blame/sin that I put on myself. Because of that blame, I started thinking that I should kill myself by running into oncoming traffic. There would be no blame if I committed suicide. As I grew up as a Christian only superficially, I knew God only with my head, not my spirit. So whenever I experienced problems, my solution was thinking of death. That was the way of darkness.

However, God is so good to me for delivering me from that darkness. Praise our Lord and Savior. When I began reading the Bible with hunger, God spoke to me with Psalm 32:1, "Blessed is the one whose transgressions are forgiven, whose sins are covered," and I felt free from sin. I started to understand that, by the blood of Jesus Christ, all my sins are covered. I am free and can be a righteous person before God. I declared and accepted Jesus as my Savior.

When I sang the song "Filled with the Holy Spirit," I knew that day that I was born again in Christ. I believe that God let me experience all these things not in vain but to know his goodness.

> **RESPONDING WITH PRAYER:**
>
> 1. Please pray for people in Myanmar struggling with suicidal thoughts. Pray for the Holy Spirit to meet them where they are and provide strength, clarity, and breakthrough.
>
> 2. Ask God to help you identify the lies you currently believe about yourself or about who he is. Pray for God to uproot those lies and replace them with his truth.

"When I was very sick for a month with trouble breathing, I told God that I didn't want to die yet, and I still wanted to serve in missions, work with [a Christian international nongovernmental organization], and be with my family. I told him, 'I believe you can give me new lungs because there is nothing you can't do.' Now I have recovered, and I believe that God has given me new lungs. Amen!"

—Myanmar national

FOR DEEPER REFLECTION:

1. What do we do when we don't see the healing we want to see, in the time frame we want to see it? How can we position our hearts and trust in God's character to sustain us in the midst of emotional or physical pain?

2. Who or what do you ultimately credit when you do experience or see healing? How can we be quicker to acknowledge God's provision (delivered through any number of avenues) and express gratitude?

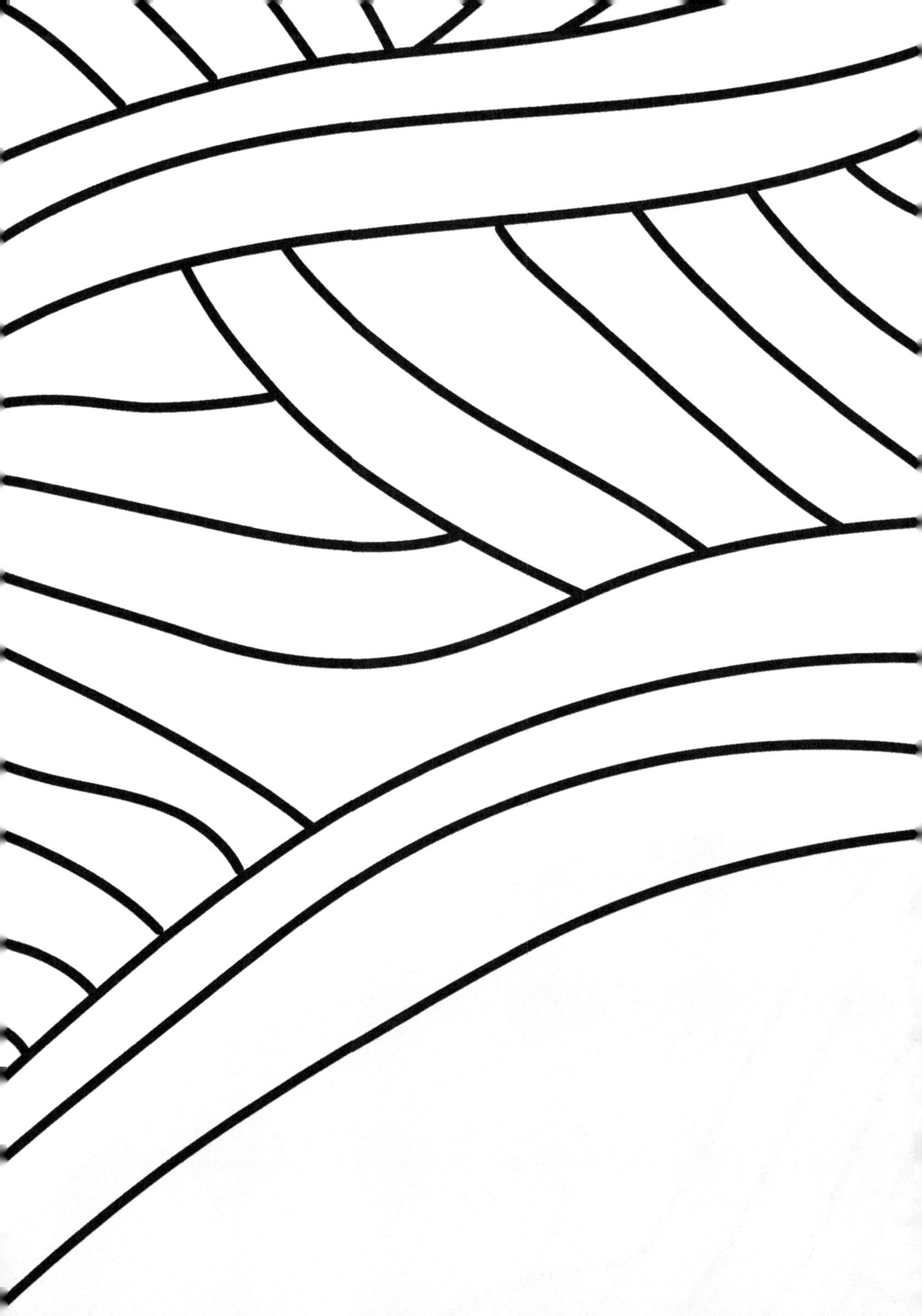

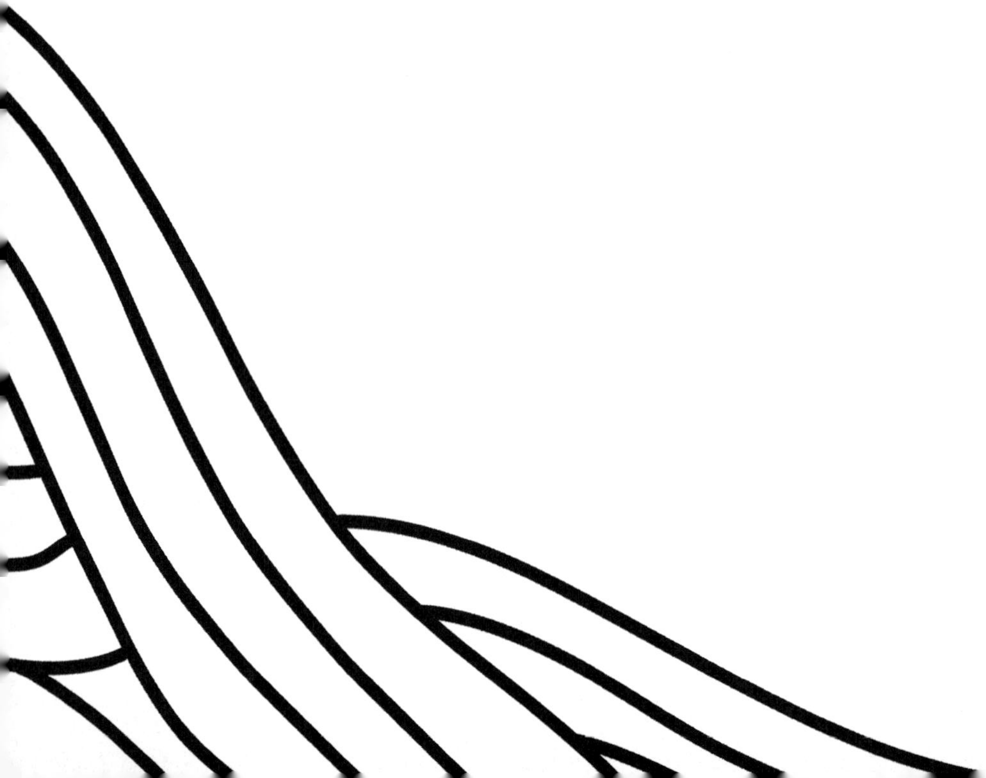

TAKEN BACK TO THE GARDEN

I am taken back to the Garden
When I try to seek Your face
The Garden where You fall on Your knees
The heartfelt cry
The tears of blood and
The anxiousness
What kind of torment have you suffered?
What kind of hurt have you known?
All because of my sins
You have suffered for my good
I saw every one of Your tears in this Garden
A sign of love was sent from Heaven
I have met it face to face
My burdens and brokenness are gone
In His touch
Something good, something kind has come
down to rescue this troubled soul
I see the hope in the glimpse of Your face
I feel the peace in Your presence again
When I'm taken back to the Garden

—D. R. Par

DUNES

Noun. Harsh terrain consisting of mounds of sand in a prolonged, repetitive pattern; a monotonous routine; a territory that is difficult to traverse.

The Lord will guide you always; he will satisfy your needs in a sun-scorched land and will strengthen your frame. You will be like a well-watered garden, like a spring whose waters never fail.

—Isaiah 58:11

"There are [many] explosions, especially around government buildings and some banks and a lot of robberies in the city, and the security forces [have] detained people without any reason. These are our challenges when we go out."

—Myanmar national

"Many people lost their jobs, and they don't have money to pay for food or rent. There are some families who are starving, and some have gone days without food to eat."

—Myanmar national

RAPIDS

Noun. The speedy and forceful part of a river as the water overcomes large obstacles and difficult terrain.

Throughout the COVID-19 pandemic and political storm in Myanmar, God is still moving. As a medical doctor and a person with strong political convictions, I am determined to serve my nation to the fullest with everything I have in me, even amid all the uncertainty.

On February 1, 2021, Myanmar entered another season of political turmoil due to a military coup, and the citizens were desperate to restore justice across the country. Thousands upon thousands of civilians across the country peacefully walked the streets in protest, demanding the restoration of the elected government. Having lived through a previous era of military dictatorship in Myanmar, it devastated me to learn that my beloved nation was once again subject to the bitter bullying of its own armed forces.

On the very first day of the political crisis in Myanmar, in that fateful month of February 2021, I asked God to provide me with his strength and decided to medically assist my people in Yangon if they ever faced danger while voicing the truth. The intensity of the protesting escalated. I took full responsibility as medic-in-charge for a free ambulance service in order to protect and give medical assistance to protesters in Yangon. There were security forces tightly controlling the activities of the medical teams who were helping the demonstrators, but we did our best to provide medical support for the enthusiastic civilians. When the security forces of the military used live ammunition to crack down on protesters, we had to step back for our own safety.

However, as a medical doctor, I was fully aware of the potential for deaths due to massive bleeding and lack of first-aid knowledge among the people, as the military shot at innocent citizens. I wasted no time teaching first aid to activist groups all across the city, training almost forty groups in how to stop bleeding and provide cardiopulmonary resuscitation (CPR). I customized the first-aid curriculum for those groups, based on the theory and skills I gained from life-support training in Jakarta, Indonesia. I offered training free of charge to anyone, regardless of race or religion. I was only able to do these things through Christ who strengthens me. He provided me with the courage to impart my medical knowledge to save lives amid the threats of the soldiers that were imprisoning citizens.

I did not halt my efforts at that point. The protests and demonstrations almost came to an end in mid-2021, when an unprecedented third wave of the COVID-19 global pandemic struck Myanmar. The vaccine came in limited supply, and the political turmoil made it even harder to access. Most doctors and nurses were afraid of the virulence of the disease without the vaccination, and there were few privately and government-funded COVID centers in the country. I myself was not vaccinated and had little experience treating COVID, but I was determined to help COVID patients.

I created my own medical response team composed of a male nurse assistant and myself as a doctor. We risked the challenging disease and made home visits and gave treatments without fear to the COVID patients. At the conclusion of the fatal third wave of COVID in Myanmar, we had saved the lives of more than five hundred people on the verge of death, including the lives of my own parents.

At present, I am still helping internally displaced people (IDPs) in states across the country that are severely affected by armed conflict following the military takeover of 2021. I frequently visit villages hosting IDPs and regularly send needed medications, in spite of the threat of detection and severe punishment from the military.

I'm confident in saying that I have tried to work hard for my country. At the same time, I am thankful to God that he provides me with all the strength I need to carry out this work. Myanmar still requires assistance in all aspects, and I have promised my Lord that I will continue doing all I can to make a positive change in my country.

> **RESPONDING WITH PRAYER:**
>
> 1. Please pray for continued courage and perseverance for the brave medical professionals providing care to people in Myanmar in the midst of conflict.
>
> 2. Is God asking you to do something that is challenging? Take time to pray for courage and strength to do the right thing, whether it be in the present or the future.

RIVULET

Noun. A small, sometimes imperceptible, trickle of water; the lasting imprint created by a small stream of water.

I am a mother of two lovely daughters, and we live together with my husband and my mother-in-law. I am so blessed to be able to share about God's miracles in my life. I would like to tell you a few testimonies of God's goodness. My journey in faith started when I was young, and my mother would bring me to church every week. I wore a beautiful dress each time and attended Sunday school with my sister. Normally I would fall asleep next to my mom during the Sunday service. My Sunday school teachers would give us Bible verses every week, and one day, on the way back home from Sunday school, I had an idea that I would memorize one of those verses and then follow that verse. I could really put the verses into practice.

When I was thirteen, I was able to participate in a fellowship program between churches. It was held every Friday evening at 6 p.m. I attended the program every week and was encouraged by listening to the testimonies of others. One week, I felt my body become cold, and I got a strange feeling. I asked my church leaders about it, and they said it happened because of the Holy Spirit's touch. They encouraged me not to be afraid and to share the testimony. Starting the following week, I felt courageous enough to speak in public and share in front of other people how God helped me solve my problems and challenges. I got strength from God with Philippians 4:13 ("I can do all this through him who gives me strength") and Proverbs 1:33 ("But whoever listens to me will live in safety and be at ease, without fear of harm"). By participating in the fellowship program, I got into the habit of kneeling in prayer and practicing fasting.

I also would like to share how God supported me with my education. As I did not have a good foundation in my education, I failed the matriculation (university entrance) exam in my first year. I took the exam two more times and finally passed it in my third year. During that year, I had to look after an elderly individual during the day and return back to the hostel where I stayed at night to study for the exam. But with God's support, I did not give up or lose hope. My mom helped me take care of the elderly individual whenever she was free. After passing the matriculation exam, I really wanted to be a degree holder. I prayed, giving my request to God. I traveled fifty miles from home to my university daily for two years. By the grace of God, during my final year, I lived at my grandfather's home in Yangon, which was closer to the university. God answered my prayer, and I got my degree majoring in international relations.

Not long after my university graduation, I had to look after my father, who suffered day and night from colon cancer. By God's preparation, we had money for my father's medical fees from selling gold that my mom had saved and support from my sister who worked abroad. My brother and I were able to assist my father, taking care of him around the clock. At the same time, we were able to build a new house. After one and a half years, my dad passed away. However, our family remained united and cared for each other well during a difficult time. I felt that this was the result of having parents who loved God. My father chose Psalm 127:1 as the motto of our home and wrote it down: "Unless the Lord builds the house, the builders labor in vain. Unless the Lord watches over the city, the guards stand watch in vain."

My last testimony of God's goodness is about how he provided for my family through financial difficulty. I experienced this through my beautiful wedding when my sister gifted me with a significant amount of money, which greatly blessed my husband and me. Later, during the COVID-19 pandemic, my husband lost his job. For our family's livelihood and to look after my two daughters, I started a small kindergarten. God blessed us so much that we had to stop accepting children because we did not have enough space. I would like to conclude my testimony with Jeremiah 17:7–8: "But blessed is the one who trusts in the Lord, whose confidence is in him. They will be like a tree planted by the water that sends out its roots by the stream. It does not fear when heat comes; its leaves are always green."

> **RESPONDING WITH PRAYER:**
>
> 1. The author mentions Jeremiah 17:7–8. Take time to reflect on this and pray for people in Myanmar to recognize God's faithfulness in their everyday lives and feel encouraged.
>
> 2. Think of the small ways God has been faithful to you in your daily life. Take time to thank him for these blessings.

CONVERGENCE

Noun. The intersection of two or more sources of water, resulting in an increase in volume and/or force.

My name is Ma Nu. I would first like to give thanks to God for his guidance and presence throughout the chaotic situation in Myanmar. By the grace of God, I had the opportunity to work for a health project that focused on promoting safe and healthy motherhood in Southeast Myanmar for an international NGO (nongovernmental organization). I would like to share my thoughts on how the resources, experiences, and other members of that organization have shaped me now.

Although I had experience working in nongovernment and humanitarian assistance organizations in Myanmar, I realized that the working environment in this particular organization was pleasant, as described in Psalm 133:1: "How good and pleasant it is when God's people live together in unity!" My line managers were gracious and patient with me. Our country director always treated all staff members equally, with no bias, and paid attention to the spiritual growth of the staff. The members of the senior management team were like God's servant leaders.

This organization did not leave Myanmar after the military coup, and our health program had been operating for around two years at the time of the COVID-19 pandemic and the coup. During this time, the program faced challenges, both expected and unexpected. Our country office provided helpful support for staff, such as security training, an encouraging Bible study on Luke, and logistical assistance and troubleshooting for the purchase and delivery of bulk amounts of medicine. Later on, after the organization had to close its office in Myanmar, these experiences equipped me to endure the job I would have next. I thank God for his timing.

I am now working in one local organization that provides emergency health assistance along the Thai border area. I was selected because of my work experience with the previous international organization and my past work with ethnic health organizations in Myanmar. Our country has a long history of armed conflict, and I had heard about camps in different states in Myanmar, which formed when people had to flee their homes. The community members I worked with had left their homes and were currently staying in bamboo shelters. It had taken them more than five days, traveling in life-threatening conditions, to reach the camp. This large camp had resulted from the coup in 2021. This was my first trip to an internally displaced persons camp, and my heart broke after hearing of their travels and witnessing their living conditions.

During morning devotions in my previous organization, I was encouraged by testimonies and messages shared by team members. I still remember a message shared by our health program manager about resilience, which encouraged me to keep going when I faced difficulties. One Bible verse that stood out to me from that message was Romans 5:3–5: "Not only so, but we also glory in our sufferings, because we know that suffering produces perseverance; perseverance, character; and character, hope. And hope does not put us to shame, because God's love has been poured out into our hearts through the Holy Spirit, who has been given to us."

Finally, I would like to share a Bible verse that gives me strength, Jeremiah 31:16: "'Restrain your voice from weeping and your eyes from tears, for your work will be rewarded,' declares the Lord." According to the history of our country, some border camps have existed for more than four decades, and my prayer is that, through God in his timing, future generations will come back safely to our native land of Myanmar.

RESPONDING WITH PRAYER:

1. Please pray for protection over local Myanmar organizations seeking to provide communities with assistance in the current conflict.

2. Reflect on a time when God prepared you in one season of your life for another. Ask him to prepare you now for the next season ahead.

"Banks are closed, and the only way to withdraw cash is to make an appointment. We have to line up in order to book an appointment date. I slept on the road, waiting thirteen hours in front of the bank in order to have a place in line. We can only withdraw a maximum of 200,000 MMK (approximately 140 USD). It has forced a lot of people to use money agents in order to get cash. These agents charge an additional 5–10 percent of the total cost."[1]

—Myanmar national

---

[1] *Please note that this quote was collected in 2021 and currency exchange rates continue to fluctuate.*

SPRING

Noun. A source of fresh water that gives life to the surrounding environment; the potential to disrupt or change the state of the land.

I would like to thank God first for giving me a chance to share about his goodness and my journey with him. My name is Shwe Min Hla. I am fifty-three years old, and I was born into a Buddhist family. At the age of twelve, I wore a Buddhist robe as a novice, and at the age of twenty-three, I was ordained as a *bhikkhu*.[1] My parents are nominal Buddhists, but I studied Buddhism myself and followed the practice. As my house was very close to a well-known pagoda, I went there every Sunday. Meditating, counting beads, and sharing blessings by reciting Buddha's words made me feel very peaceful. I paid homage day and night at home during the other days of the week.

However, one of my weaknesses is that I am short-tempered, and back then, I often fought with others. If something made me angry, I would feel content only after I got revenge. Sometimes, on my way back home from the pagoda, cars would pass by and splash muddy water onto me, and I would follow them on my bicycle and swear at them. At that time, the road conditions in Yangon were bad with many potholes. Sometimes I thought, *I've just finished meditating in the pagoda and blessing others—how can I react this way?* But I could not control my anger.

I passed my days being religious on one hand and getting angry, fighting, gambling, and drinking on the other. One day, my Christian girlfriend's friend shared the gospel with me. I was thirty-four at that time. I quarreled with that person as I considered my religion to be the truth and the best. Not long after that incident, my girlfriend invited me to go to church with her. I worked at a restaurant, and she knew that it was very busy on Sundays. I gently explained that I could not take leave on busy days but that

---
1 *A Buddhist monk*

I would go with her when I was not busy. However, in my mind, I thought, *I don't want anything to do with your church. Why should I go with you?* For two years I remained that way. Then, suddenly, I was let go from that restaurant. My girlfriend had not forgotten my words, and she reminded me, "Now that you don't have any work this Sunday, come to church with me." I was dejected and wanted to keep my promise, so I followed her to church.

When I was at church, many strangers warmly welcomed me. I had never met them before. Later, I would come to know that they had been praying for me for the previous two years because my girlfriend had asked them to. Not long after that, I got a new job. I attended church weekly, as I no longer had to work on Sundays. After attending weekly Bible studies, I had many thoughts. My religion at that time taught me to do good things so I could go to a good place in my next life. Conversely, I believed that if I did bad things, I would go to a bad place in my next life. However, Jesus knew the people he created were not always able to do good things even though they knew what was right and kept living in sin, so he gave his own life and allowed himself to be crucified to save them.

I started to reflect on myself and saw that even though I was paying homage for around two hours per day, I was doing many bad things in the remaining time. Another thing I came to understand was that even though my religion was good, if I was not able to follow its rules, my efforts were worthless. That is why, finally, I invited Jesus Christ who rescued me from sin to be my personal Lord and Savior. Jesus saved me only because of his unfailing love, not because of my goodness or the good things I did. Frankly speaking, I accepted Jesus in my life, as I realized it was impossible for me to "be good" by myself, and I knew I needed grace. Looking back, it was perplexing that I lost my job at the restaurant after working there for ten years without any problems or mistakes. I couldn't understand why they let me go. However, now I can see how God used that to bring me closer to him.

After I received Jesus Christ, I experienced a breakthrough in a deep-seated fear of mine. Ever since I was young, I had never been able to stand up and speak in front of a large group of people. If I had to do it, I would start to shake, and my voice wouldn't come out. One day, my pastor asked me to share at church the testimony of how I came to know Jesus. Suddenly, my whole body felt heavy and flushed. I told her I didn't think I could do it. My pastor and friends encouraged and prayed for me, asking God to prepare me. As I had no way to reject the request, I just went along with it. When the speaker called me to share my testimony that day, I walked to the pulpit with heavy steps. However, when I touched the mic to speak, the fear I had been harboring for my whole life was nowhere to be found, and I was able to share my testimony steadily. This is a miracle that God has done.

I got baptized on October 2, 2005. Later, I realized that my faith at that time came only from my mind and not yet my heart or my actions. There were many changes in my life. But God has the best plan for his loved ones. He molded me step by step. Even though my family was not rich, we were living comfortably. I did not know what poverty was, and I never sympathized with the poor. But God sent me to the impoverished and made me learn what poverty means. The place where God sent me was one of the villages where people were living in bamboo shelters with no electricity, no phone service, and no job, and they depended on donated food. They did not know the Burmese language very well and only spoke the Karen language. It was so hard for me to communicate at first. Before this, I had lived in an urban area and had just come back from Japan. The living standard there was totally different for me. Life became very rough, and I started to understand and empathize with the poor and started to love them.

After I experienced many difficulties, God started to work in my heart in 2009. I wanted to share God's goodness all the time. I thirsted for God's words and read the Bible throughout my free time. The Holy Spirit led me and helped me to understand scriptures that I hadn't understood before. There were so many times when I received answers to questions I had been contemplating after opening my Bible or through pastors coming and explaining to me the very thing I had been wondering about.

As I wanted to know more about God, I attended a small evangelist school. Because the school was small, there were insufficient teachers and learning materials. As the school motto was "Five Loaves and Two Fish," we had to pray at least two hours per day and read five Bible chapters. Bible study was in the morning, and in the afternoon we went out to share the gospel. After attending for six months, I was asked by the school to assist in one of the training sessions. I did not want to go, as I did not know anything about the training, but when I read my Bible at night, God spoke to me with Isaiah 48:11: "For my own sake, for my own sake, I do this. How can I let myself be defamed? I will not yield my glory to another." The message that came to my heart was that God would do it for his name and glory; I only needed to accept the opportunity and go.

I was assured that I wouldn't feel condemned, as I was going in his name. I knew the victory belonged to him. At night, I dreamed that a pastor with a white shirt whom I did not know came and put his hand on my head and prayed for me. When morning came, I let my wife know about it and went to the training. God gave me many new experiences and taught me many lessons there. I praised God's name and started to participate more fully in God's mission in similar ways.

In 2017, God called me to be his full-time servant, and I served at a church while also completing my master's in divinity at a theological institute. Now I am serving as an assistant pastor. I am very grateful to God that he not only saved me through his miracles but also let me serve in his mission. May the highest name of God be glorified.

RESPONDING WITH PRAYER:

1. Please pray for open hearts and opportunities for people in Myanmar who don't yet know Jesus to experience real relationship with him.

2. Think of people in your life who currently don't know Jesus. Ask God to provide you with wisdom and opportunities to convey his love in ways that are meaningful to them.

EBB

Verb. The action of water when it pulls away to return to its source.

I felt God's grace when I took the matriculation (university entrance) exam. It was an important time for every student. My friends went to a fortune teller to help them pass the exam. They rented a car and went to one of the most well-known monks to perform incantations over their materials—the pens, pencils, and other stationery that they would use in the exam. Even though they told me to do it too, I didn't agree. They said that, even if I could not go with them, I should send along my materials and a donation for the monk, but I chose not to do it. I said in my mind to God, "I just rely on you, God. I don't believe in anything other than You, Lord." I believed that, because of God, no matter what kinds of questions would be asked, I would be able to answer them successfully. In reality, there were subjects on the exam that I didn't have confidence about passing. However, I didn't think I would fail. I believed that God would provide his best for me. There was no doubt in my belief. In the end, I passed the matriculation exam.

We have many difficulties in our lives. There are so many tempting ways to solve our problems. We need to trust in the Lord and have absolute faith without doubt in prayer.

> **RESPONDING WITH PRAYER:**
>
> 1. Please pray for encouragement for students in Myanmar, and for continued opportunities for education, as so many schools have shut down.
>
> 2. Think about areas in your life where your spiritual integrity could be challenged. Ask God for renewed strength and commitment to stay faithful to him.

DEEP

Adjective. Extending far below the surface.

I serve in a church in a border town in Thailand, and I would like to share about how I've experienced God's love. I first heard about the gospel message through one of my teachers, who said that Jesus died on the cross for our sins and was resurrected on the third day. I heard that if I believed in that, I would be in heaven with him when I died. At the time, I didn't believe what I heard.

One day, while we were reading the Bible, God spoke to me. It frightened me when I realized that I couldn't work my way into heaven, that it didn't matter how many good things I did; it would never be enough. Even though I knew that, it didn't change me. Then, one day, God spoke to me again. In the Bible, when Jesus called Peter, he followed immediately. And when God spoke to me, he said, "I'm calling you. Why aren't you following me?" At that time, I thought, *Ohhh . . . God loves me that much*, and I started to believe in God.

There have been many times when I have truly seen and felt God's presence in my life. I am easily affected by my emotions and easily feel sad. It hurt me when I felt that the people who I loved didn't love me or when I felt abandoned. Although I was sad in my heart, I praised God in song. When I praised God, he spoke to me and said, "Whenever you are sad, whenever you are in despair, I am with you. Emmanuel, the God who is always with you, loves you. When people don't want to listen to you, I will always listen to you." When God spoke to me like that, it made me so happy that I found myself in tears. Since then, whatever I do and no matter how I feel, I just talk to God.

RESPONDING WITH PRAYER:

1. Please pray for Myanmar believers to experience God's love at an intimate level.

2. Have there been times in your life when you've felt that God has spoken to you in an intimate and personal way? Take time to thank him for his deep and personal love and prayerfully consider ways to slow down and make space for his companionship.

STEADY

Adjective. Consistent and stable, as in a flow of water.

First of all, I would like to thank you for the opportunity to share this testimony about God's goodness. Thank you for the opportunity to participate in this book. My name is Naw Lar May. I am a Myanmar national living in Dubai with my husband and my children. My husband worked in a hotel, and we had to move to Dubai from Myanmar with the whole family because of his job. My husband's current income was just enough for our daughter's school fees, the family's food, and other household expenses. Our son was about to go to school, but we did not have enough to cover his school fees. My husband was offered an opportunity to change jobs, which would help us cover our son's school fees. However, when I spent time with God, I asked him, "Should my husband change his job or not?" God spoke to me with Hebrews 13:5-6: "Keep your lives free from the love of money and be content with what you have, because God has said, 'Never will I leave you; never will I forsake you.' So we say with confidence, 'The Lord is my helper; I will not be afraid. What can mere mortals do to me?'"

I didn't pressure my husband to accept the job offer because I felt it was best not to choose the job based on money alone. My husband also didn't want to take this new job, so I agreed with him to not pursue it. Although we didn't know God's plan, we simply obeyed his word. By God's grace, my husband got a salary increase at his current job when my son was about to start school. The increased salary was more than double the amount of the salary he would've been paid if he had changed to the new job! After meditating on God's word that says, "Keep your lives free from the love of money," and then following what we believed God was asking us to do by not accepting the job offer, we felt the promise of God: "Never will I leave you; never will I forsake you." As the psalmist said, "Your word is a lamp for my feet, a light on my path" (Psalm 119:105). I have actually felt that our difficulties have been smoothed out because I followed his words completely in these situations.

The apartment where we currently live is supported by my husband's employer. Unexpectedly, we were told that we had to move from it by the end of the month because the building had to be renovated. The employer said that he would later reimburse us for the expenses, but we would initially have to pay out of pocket. Then, we received a new announcement that we had to move everything before the end of the month, which was even earlier than originally expected. We were so worried because we only had 4,000 AED (approximately 1,089 USD) for health insurance and 500 AED (approximately 136 USD) for other costs. Alarmed, I cried and prayed all night. At that time, I received a letter from two friends offering to help me with money and other assistance if I needed it. I really gave thanks to God that there were people who really cared about us. I told them that if I really needed it, I would let them know.

When I spent time with God, he spoke to me with another part of Hebrews 13:5, which says, "Be content with what you have." After meditating on this verse, I decided to wait for God's timing, and I did not borrow money, believing that God would protect and provide for me. Before the end of the month, God prepared one room in our current housing compound for 4,000 AED per month. The room was convenient for our family of four, so I thanked God and signed a one-month contract. Renting an apartment on a monthly basis is unusual, as a three-month contract with a high deposit is typically required in Dubai. The fact that we could sign a one-month contract was another blessing from God.

Because of God's protection, we did not need to move to a different housing compound, which would have required us to take out a loan, and we were able to financially stand on our own without worries. If we had taken on debt and moved to a different place, we would have struggled even more and worried every day. Most of our friends have been anxious and worried about paying off their loans. I thank the Holy Spirit for leading me to commit our needs to God and to take refuge and follow his words in Proverbs 3:5-6: "Trust in the Lord with all your heart and lean not on your own understanding; in all your ways submit to him, and he will make your paths straight."

My God, whom I worship, is a living God, and he answers when I call him. He is always ready to help us with our tough situations, difficulties, and worries. God so loved each of us that he gave his only begotten Son for us. I pray that all believers may be strengthened by approaching him in prayer, walking with obedience, and holding on to his promises. Amen.

RESPONDING WITH PRAYER:

1. Please pray for Myanmar nationals who are working in other countries and are separated from their homes and families.

2. Sometimes it's difficult to see the whole path forward through a situation. Ask God to show you what the next right thing to do is within a current challenge you are facing.

"It has been really challenging to be a Christian father in Myanmar at this time. My family and I have faced many difficulties because of Myanmar's economic deterioration and widespread conflict. However, I put my trust in God's provision as I continue to do my best to care for my family. I will not give up because I trust that God will remain faithful."

—Myanmar national

FOR DEEPER REFLECTION:

1. Do you feel that it's hard to thank God for the small things while waiting for the big things? If so, why?

2. What is the value of thanking God for the small things? What happens when we thank God?

3. Most of our lives are contained in daily routines that may feel mundane. How can we still appreciate what God is doing in these moments? How can we establish rhythms of gratitude in the midst of the ordinary?

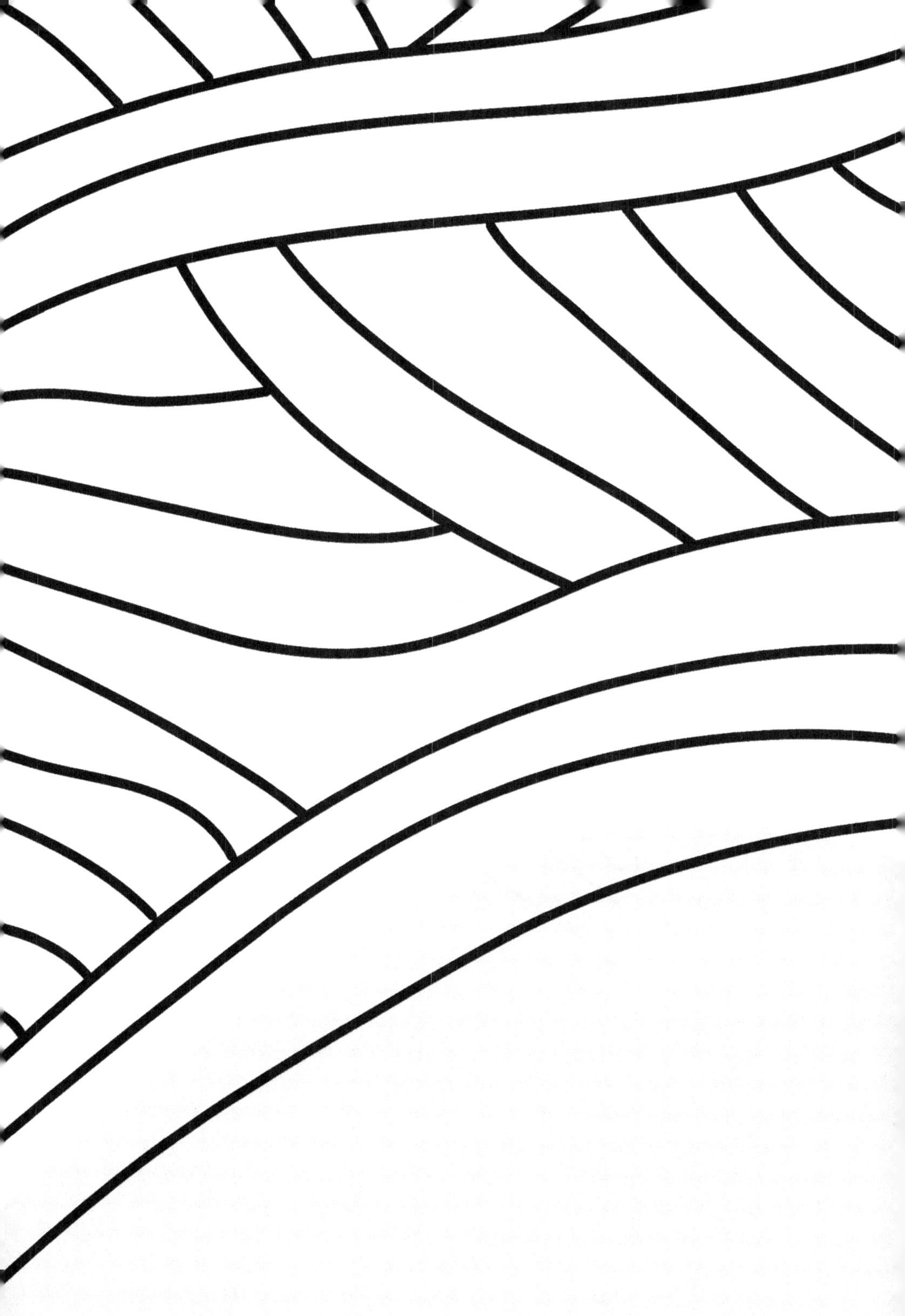

WILDERNESS

Noun. A barren, lonely place; no way out as far as the eye can see.

How long, Lord? Will you forget me forever? How long will you hide your face from me? How long must I wrestle with my thoughts and day after day have sorrow in my heart? How long will my enemy triumph over me? Look on me and answer, Lord my God. Give light to my eyes, or I will sleep in death, and my enemy will say, "I have overcome him," and my foes will rejoice when I fall. But I trust in your unfailing love; my heart rejoices in your salvation. I will sing the Lord's praise, for he has been good to me.

—Psalm 13

"Our plans and dreams have now been limited as if we are living in a jail, and it affects our mental well-being."

—Myanmar national

"Depression and suicide among the youth in our community is so heartbreaking."

—Myanmar national

DROP

Noun. An unsatisfactory, miniscule amount of water; of seemingly limited utility.

First of all, I would like to praise God for his grace. I never thought I would ever be in this place called a refugee camp. We ran away from the war and took shelter in a small village. At that time, an uncle who was in the refugee camp called me and encouraged me to join him there. So, after discussing it together, some of my relatives, a few other villagers, and I decided to go. It was not a great situation because we did not have much money, but God prepared everything, and we arrived safely. After a day, people came to give us food and clothes. After a week, around one thousand people had arrived. At that time, the pastor and church members discussed the situation and made preparations to feed and clothe us.

As the months passed, it became difficult for us refugees as well as the people hosting us. People in other countries donated as much as they could, and eventually we were able to receive food rations. However, some were unable to receive enough rations and struggled to find food. There also weren't many jobs. Those hosting refugees in their homes felt sorry for us, and those of us who came and stayed with them felt sorry for our hosts. There were forty people who came and lived with my uncle, and as there were a lot of us, sometimes there was tension. However, we had enough to eat and a safe place to live. There are also many Christian teachers and nurses here who willingly provide their services. We are very grateful for the good education and the affordable hospital fees.

When I arrived, I thought I would only stay two months and then be able to return home, but now the situation is getting worse, and it is not safe to go back. I miss my parents and siblings—I miss my village—the longing for home and family has overwhelmed me. That's why I always feel unhappy. This is not my home, so there are many challenges to navigate that add to my unease. I always feel sad when I think back to the time when I was with my whole family and my friends in the village. Right now, we are all separated due to the political unrest. Sometimes I worry that I will never be with my family and loved ones again. I always think about going back home even though it is not safe to stay in my village. Then, even if I die, I will die with my family; if I live, we will all live together. Even though I can live safely here in the refugee camp, I am unhappy and full of anxiety. Therefore, I am always praying that the situation will get better soon and that I will be able to see my family and loved ones again. I am praying that I will be able to work in service for God as I did before.

RESPONDING WITH PRAYER:

1. Please pray for Myanmar individuals and families who have been displaced or separated and are living in other people's homes, refugee camps, or IDP camps. Please pray for encouragement for this Myanmar author specifically as she faces anxiety and longs to be with her family and home community.

2. Have you ever been in a season of limbo and uncertainty? Take time to prayerfully reflect on how God sustained you in that season and used it to prepare you for the season ahead.

"During the past few years, we have lost a few friends in the casualties, and it has affected both my mental and physical well-being. Seeing lots of IDPs (internally displaced people) and their tragic moments really makes me feel exhausted since I never experienced these kinds of events in my life before. Sometimes I wonder if I should leave everything behind and just disappear or run away from the current situation and give up. However, we are grateful that we have friends and people that encourage and remember us in their prayers. We can feel God's protection and provision in times of hardship."

—Myanmar national

"We struggle with depression, loneliness, anxiety, and hopelessness. Some of my friends were arrested because they joined protests. Some of my friends passed away. It's very hard for me to say 'Rest in peace' to their families every day."

—Myanmar national

THIRST

Verb. To desire or long for water.
Noun. The physical response to prolonged periods of drought.

My name is Maw Nu, and today is my twenty-eighth birthday. I would like to thank God for allowing me to live until the age of twenty-eight during this very difficult time. This birthday will be marked with the memory of writing about the situation of our country and the difficulties experienced by our people. I will express not only my feelings but also the feelings of people who are fleeing the war in various parts of Myanmar.

In this time of crisis, everyone is exhausted, not only physically but also mentally. There are many people who lost their family members due to COVID-19, and many people lost their lives and property because of the unjust killings and torture by the military. There are also many IDPs who migrated and left their homes due to the war and the orders of the military council. It was painful for them to leave the homes that they carefully saved money for over many years and built with their own sweat and blood. Even though I am not in a situation where I have to leave my home, tears burn my eyes when I hear that people are moving to other villages. I cannot imagine how tiring it is for the people who have to relocate.

Livelihoods have become very difficult to maintain, and it is risky for people who have to move to other villages to live. For those who have continued to work in their home villages but have had to flee to a different place, it is dangerous for them to go back and forth. Some people have been killed in the crossfire when they went back to their village to harvest rice and bring back food. I cannot imagine how painful and heartbreaking it is for the family members left behind. At this time of national instability and difficulty, the price of goods has increased sharply, and it makes it difficult, not only for people who have moved but also for people who have stayed in their homes. Some have lost all hope and committed suicide. It is clear that many people are suffering from significant emotional damage and exhaustion.

If we look at health, there are also many people who have lost their lives because of transportation difficulties that prevented them from receiving the medical care they needed. For education, the sector is declining, as many schools have had to close or are inaccessible. Therefore, children who are old enough to study cannot study and have few healthy and productive ways to spend their time, which can harm their futures.

Most people living in Myanmar suffer from mental fatigue, exhaustion, worry, physical health issues, and educational delays. We cannot even think about the future and plan in advance; we are aimless. Therefore, I am writing this to ask you to remember us in your prayers and please send encouragement to us.

RESPONDING WITH PRAYER:

1. The author requests prayer for people in Myanmar suffering from mental fatigue, exhaustion, worry, physical health issues, and educational delays. Please spend time praying for one of these issues.

2. Have you ever been in a season where the future seemed hopeless? Take time to identify moments or times in that season when God showed up in big or small ways.

"From my own experiences of being a mother, raising a young child in the current environment is stressful for daily living. There are not enough vaccines or [the cost] is too expensive, and we cannot get proper medical care or the medicine a child needs when they are sick because of the block on foreign transportation [imports]. Also, there are not enough doctors. Mothers on the front line are even more challenged physically and psychologically, as they witness shootings and unspeakable violence and endure daily trauma. This has impacted those pregnant or hoping to be pregnant, and miscarriage has risen highly over the past two years.

Even for me—I wanted to die when I was pregnant. I feel guilty, too, because if I hadn't been pregnant, I would have joined one of the ethnic armed groups for sure. I feel defeated, like I cannot do anything. People I know have passed away, run away, hidden, lost connections, gone to jail, and have become separated from family because of military fighting. Mothers suffer even more for their children, as some are killed and some are separated.

God reminds me to embrace myself and to focus on him even though bad things happen in our lives. Our life is in his purpose, and living is full of meaning when we serve him. So I would like to say thank you to God for keeping me safe and alive so I can support those who need help. I have to remind myself of that when I am down, and I know... he will do what he knows is the best [for us]. Amen!"

—Myanmar national

FOR DEEPER REFLECTION:

1. In Psalm 13, the author begins with the raw expression of his emotions and ends by reminding himself who God is. Which part of this psalm resonates with you today?

How long, Lord? Will you forget me forever? How long will you hide your face from me? How long must I wrestle with my thoughts and day after day have sorrow in my heart? How long will my enemy triumph over me? Look on me and answer, Lord my God. Give light to my eyes, or I will sleep in death, and my enemy will say, "I have overcome him," and my foes will rejoice when I fall. But I trust in your unfailing love; my heart rejoices in your salvation. I will sing the Lord's praise, for he has been good to me. —Psalm 13

2. Are there thoughts or feelings that you find difficult to communicate to God? There are many examples in the book of Psalms where the author is completely transparent with God about doubt, grief, anger, and despair. In many of these psalms, the author chooses to conclude by remembering instances of God's faithfulness in the past. Wherever you're at today, take time to express your feelings to God without any filter. After you've expressed your feelings to God, take time to reflect on a past example of his faithfulness in your own life.

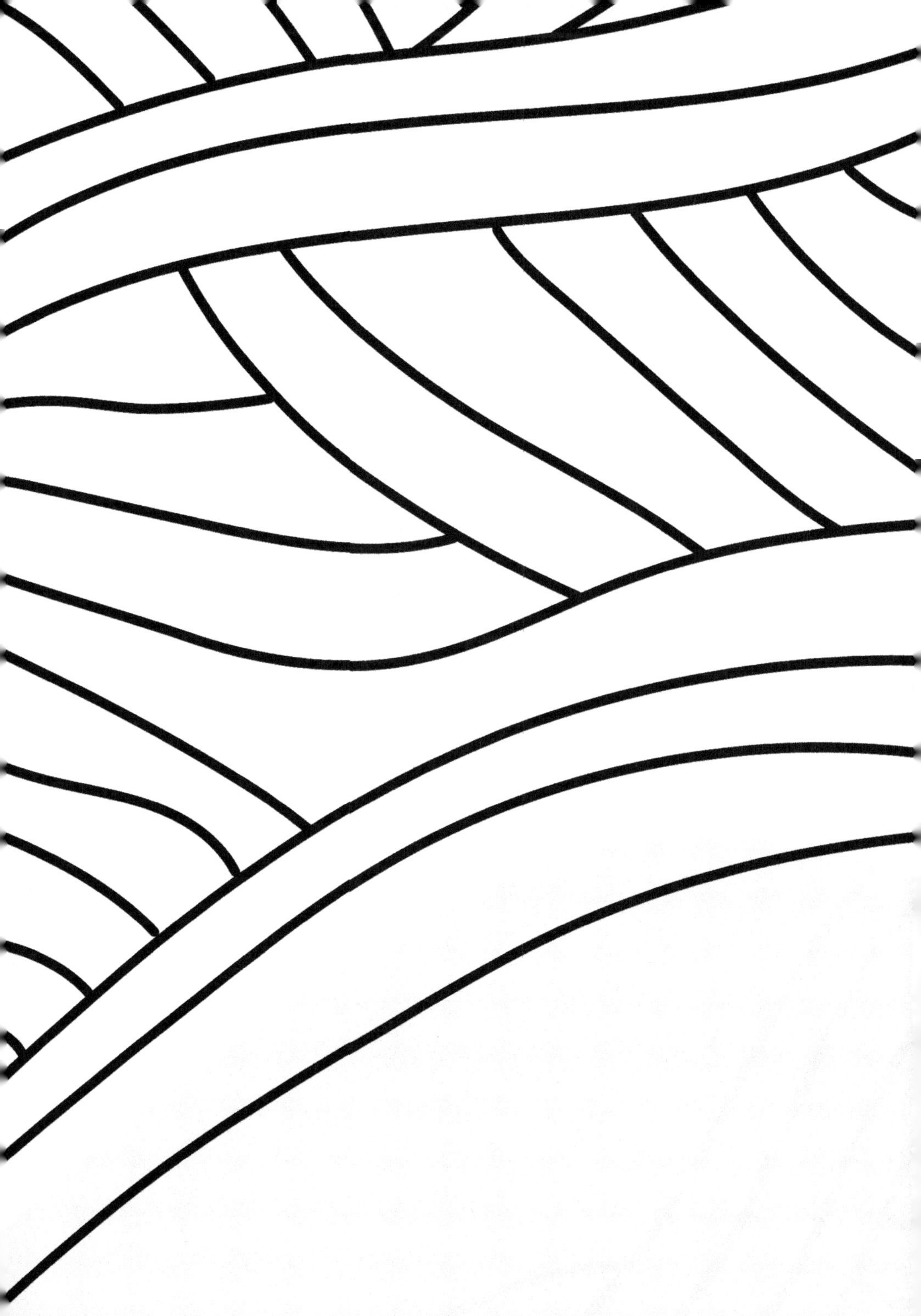

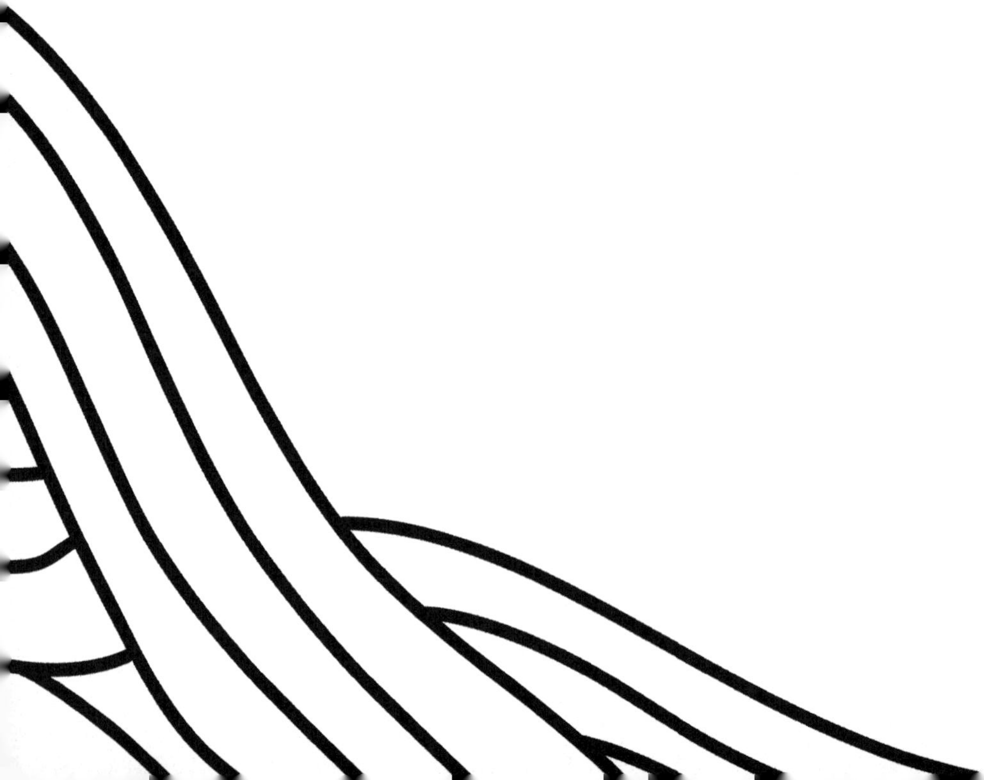

AMEN

I sat in my favorite spot
The solitude accompanied me
In a quiet and shadowy place . . .
In stillness and loneliness,
The thorn in my flesh distracted my mind,
Until I shook myself in tears
As the waves of the ocean reaching for the
shores over and over again,
My heart tossed and turned, desperate to get to
the safe shore again . . .
"Have I ever failed you yet?"
"Have I ever not fulfilled the promise I made?"
"Have I ever forsaken or forgotten you?"
A whisper came from Above once again
"Fear not for I will be with you"
My weary soul agrees, "Amen."

—D. R. Par

CANYON

Noun. A deep, expansive space that separates two sides; a seemingly insurmountable gap where access to water is out of reach.

The fortress will be abandoned, the noisy city deserted; citadel and watchtower will become a wasteland forever, the delight of donkeys, a pasture for flocks, till the Spirit is poured on us from on high, and the desert becomes a fertile field, and the fertile field seems like a forest. The Lord's justice will dwell in the desert, his righteousness live in the fertile field.

—Isaiah 32:14–16

"One quote that has been encouraging me is one you might be familiar with from Abraham Lincoln. It says, 'My concern is not whether God is on our side. My greatest concern is to be on God's side, for God is always right.' This is encouraging to me because it reminds me to stand on God's side. Even though we as humans might not like the choice, it will always be right."

—Myanmar national

"Everyone can say that God is good when it's convenient. It is difficult to say that God is good when we are facing difficulties and failures, but it is more rewarding."

—Myanmar national

CURRENT

*Noun. The pull or force of water in a certain
direction with momentum.*

In 2019, before the military coup, I served as an evangelist, taught poor children for free, and gave livelihood training and support to internally displaced people (IDPs) in Myanmar as much as I could. Even before the coup happened, I shared the gospel with them along with providing food, medicine, clothes, and health information in Rakhine and Kayin states. I'd like to share some of my journey with you and how I've seen God move.

The military coup happened in 2021, and as a result, there were many protests in the country's economic capital, Yangon. A number of people were shot and wounded by the military, and many died. When I saw all of this happen, I felt so sad. I was not able to do anything except go and comfort the families of the deceased. I asked God, "How can I help these people?" At that time, I felt God tell me to leave Yangon. I didn't have enough money, but I ended up leaving Yangon with only 70,000 kyats (approximately 33 USD), which someone had gifted to me.

There were protests across the whole country. I asked God again, "What should I do?" My fiancée was in a province far away. I went to see her, as we hadn't seen each other since the COVID pandemic began in 2020. Still, even though I was glad to see her, I did not feel happy. At that time, one of my friends suggested that I go and help internally displaced people. I didn't know what would happen in the future, but I moved forward based on how I felt God was leading me.

By the grace of God, I was able to share the gospel in remote areas where displaced people were living because of armed conflict. Even when everything was difficult, God opened doors for me. I arrived in Thailand during a difficult time with the help of an ethnic resistance group. There, I received donations from friends and was able to help IDPs in Myanmar. My friends worked for an aid organization, and they also provided medicine for the IDPs. I was able to help people in need with the help of my friends. Even though I was in trouble as well, God gave me the chance to help others. I could see that God was using me to be a blessing in people's lives.

I also saw God's movement through opportunities to share the gospel. By sharing the gospel with internally displaced people, I had a chance to live in one of the "free zones" in Myanmar—areas not under military control. I married my fiancée there, and that in itself is a testimony of God's goodness.

As I mentioned, I left Yangon with only 70,000 kyats (33 USD). I realized that as I focused on serving other people's needs more than my own, God himself took responsibility for me. My wedding ceremony became one of God's miracles; God prepared and provided for everything. While I was engaged, I traveled to the Thai border to support the IDPs there and meet with some churches that I had been serving with since 2019. When I arrived, many church members invited me to their homes to worship God together, and at that time, they generously donated money to me out of love. I hadn't expected this generosity at all, and it was such a blessing. I was in this Thai border town for thirteen days, and after ten days, I had been given enough money to cover the cost of the wedding rings.

God didn't stop providing there. After this, I went to support IDPs and stayed with one of Myanmar's ethnic resistance groups for a long time to help respond to needs there. Out of kindness, members from this ethnic resistance group gave me a generous amount of money to help with the wedding costs. Although the costs were quite high, I didn't have to borrow money from anyone to cover the expenses. When it came time for the wedding, people graciously donated chickens for the food, provided flowers for decoration, and covered transportation costs. God's way is so special. I kept working to share the gospel until two days before my wedding—and I started again two days after.

As violence increased in Myanmar, transportation became more limited because of security concerns, and it was difficult to go to different towns. For this reason, my wife and I settled again in a new town, and I organized sewing training and nurse aide training to internally displaced youth.

I didn't have any money to provide this training, but I gave all of my needs to Jesus, and he arranged everything. When I went to a night market with a friend, I met a nongovernmental organization (NGO) worker and started talking with him about the training I wanted to provide. He gave me a phone number for a local NGO that was able to help me start the training. My investments were trusting in God and stewarding this training responsibly, and God took responsibility for everything.

We gave a six-month training to twenty youth. At that time, there were many attacks and air strikes on our town from military forces, so this was a safety concern for us. Supporting the ministry was a financial concern as well. My wife and I decided to move to find employment to support the ministry, and we left for the Thai side, crossing the Thai border with 11,000 Thai baht (325 USD) in our hands—again, a gift from a friend for the cost of travel. When we arrived on the Thai side, a friend allowed us to live in his house. By the grace of God, we were able to rent a room. We lived there with only two pillows and two plates. After living there for a month, fighting broke out in the town we had been living in on the Myanmar side. Due to the fighting, civilians had to escape across the river to find refuge in Thailand—this included our youth in the sewing ministry program. I felt God say to me at that time, "This is why I sent you first so that you could comfort them." He led me to prepare things in advance for them.

As I was concerned that fighting would occur, I had purchased emergency food and hammocks back in the town we had been living in on the Myanmar side for the youth from our sewing program. However, when the actual fighting began, they did not have time to take these supplies with them; they ran away immediately. They were able to make it across the river safely, and I had to pay the guide who had helped them cross to the Thai side. It was amazing how I got the money to help the youth cross—people who I never expected to offer help and people I didn't know contacted me and sent me the money.

A total of twelve people arrived on the Thai side. I comforted them with God's word. Our God who never makes mistakes, who is always moving—he moved within our lives and ministries. Coincidentally, through one youth, I got connected with another NGO, and God provided necessary sewing materials through that organization. Youth who felt hopeless were able to access income through sewing. They also taught other people. Three of the youth decided to serve in missions and ministry.

God led me to start a church, to comfort people from Myanmar who were coming to the Thai side with physical, mental, and emotional burdens. Even though we did not have any money, we started our church, with faith, in a small room. Although it was not an official church, God worked through us. People were freed and received new revelations. The people fleeing Myanmar and seeking refuge in Thailand have a lot of trauma from running away. At this church, they are accepted by the church members as family and receive the love of God and strength to continue. Through divine appointment, I was put in contact with a Myanmar pastor from a church in Singapore and that organization provided a place for us to use as a church. To help us avoid frequent documentation checks by the authorities, they rented a place for us to live near town. Even though I don't know how long they will rent it for us, I can serve God with a relieved heart for now.

Our youth group has also been able to learn and serve God. Out of the blue, one Bible school ministry contacted me and offered to support our youth with homeschooling and an international curriculum. Now, the youth are able to continue their education. God moved for us. Moreover, every day we need to provide food for twenty people, and as of now we haven't starved.

Another amazing thing was that three youth, my wife, and I were able to receive ten-year permit cards to be in Thailand—something many people have to wait a very long time to get. We didn't even have formal identification cards, and we still received ten-year permits. May our God be glorified.

The church we started began with sixteen people, and now we have around 150 church members. We see growth. All of the people in our church are people who had to run away from Myanmar due to armed conflict and violence. We have been able to comfort, guide, and support them. I have found that God went ahead and prepared the way for us, and he also prepared the way for them. Our greatest spiritual victory was when seventeen people accepted Jesus Christ as their Lord and Savior.

God will not stop there. I am confident that God will keep his promises into the next generation, to produce spiritual fruit and be his light. May God bless you all.

RESPONDING WITH PRAYER:

1. Please pray for Myanmar churches and organizations providing assistance across Myanmar's borders. Ask God to help them as they work to obtain permission from local authorities to operate, secure funding and supplies, and face ongoing trauma along with overwhelming need that can result in staff or volunteer burnout.

2. Think back to a time in your life when you experienced lack or deficiency, whether it was material, emotional, or relational. How did God provide for you in big or small ways in the midst of that? Take time to thank God for his provision.

FLOOD

Noun. An overwhelming volume of water converging in one place and at one time, covering areas of otherwise dry ground.

I serve as an evangelist. I am a sewing teacher, and I love to share the gospel with people. Firstly, I would like to thank God, who gives me the opportunity to share my testimony. I would like to testify about God who enables us in impossible situations, God who is full of compassion and who cares for us. Three of my friends and I went to share about Jesus in a village where people didn't know him. During our trip, we were able to share the gospel with about twenty people. By the grace of God, we received donations and were able to feed them dinner, even though we ourselves didn't have enough money.

Unfortunately, when we arrived at the village, there were many elderly people and children who were sick. A member of our group was a medical professional, but there was no medicine, and we didn't have any money to buy more. However, we wrote down the name of each patient and the medicine they needed, with faith. In addition to this, there were about ten families who were starving in that village, and it broke our hearts. Again, we felt that we could not do anything, as we did not have money, but we knew we had God. The four of us prayed together to the God who can do everything.

We still didn't have money to buy medicine the next day. We prayed to God again at night, and the God who does miracles, who loves people and never fails to help, is so good. The next morning, I received an unexpected call, and the caller sent me funds. We were able to buy medicine and not only treat patients but also distribute rice to starving families. It is my testimony that when we call on God who gives us the promise "Call me, I will answer you," no matter how hard it seems, God really answers.

He is a God who does great things. He is a God who provides and never abandons us.

God bless you all.

> **RESPONDING WITH PRAYER:**
>
> 1. Please pray for Myanmar people who are in need of medicine and food. Due to the present crisis, transportation routes have been disrupted or cut off and jobs have been lost, making it difficult to access or purchase critical supplies. Ask God to provide for them as they face these challenges.
>
> 2. Can you think of any people in your life who pray persistently for the needs and well-being of others? Take time to thank God for them, and ask him to inspire you to do likewise.

SATURATE

Verb. To fully permeate an environment with water.

I praise God for his great love and mercy! God is our refuge and strength, a very present help in times of trouble! The Lord is moving in Myanmar. People hunger for the Savior of their lives, and when they hear the gospel of Jesus Christ, they accept him and rejoice. In the past, most people in the country—from the rich to the poor—refused to hear the gospel because of the stronghold of darkness covering their eyes. Now, the Lord is doing mighty things in Myanmar.

God showed me that the evil one had strongly rooted false teachings in Central Myanmar and had built up his power base there. However, the Lord also showed me that he himself had started moving in Central Myanmar. I praise God for working throughout the crisis because many people are turning back to the true God.

Recently, I came back from a town in Central Myanmar. I stayed seven days with our prayer group there, as we felt led to through revelation from the Lord. People from this town had been led astray by the devil's power. However, the Lord said to me, "I will destroy the temple of Satan and I will build my temple. I will build my church." Then, he showed me the word ARRESTED. I saw the written word in English clearly in the Spirit, like an open vision. At first I was stunned, and I wondered if any of our prayer group would be arrested. However, after I asked the Lord further, he said that he had arrested all evil powers just before our trip. According to his promise, he did.

In my spirit, I felt so peaceful and light, although there were a lot of pagodas and statues in the town. When we shared the gospel, people accepted it happily, even in their temples full of idols.

People accepted Jesus when we introduced him to them because the Lord removed the power of evil from their eyes. Praise the Lord!

The current political crisis and trouble make us rely totally on God. This crisis has tested our foundations in Christ and has required us to reflect on the authenticity of our relationship and trust in him. It has increased my knowledge of God. I have received wisdom from above and the mind of Christ to distinguish between physical and spiritual realms. My faith in Christ has increased as he has blessed me to know more of the reality of his presence in my life. I can stay peacefully in his grace. He has taught me that we are receiving a kingdom that cannot be shaken, although we are living in a shaken nation. My God is a consuming fire. His protection and provision are enough and are perfect in my life.

I see the Lord pulling down evil strongholds in the spiritual realm. In the near future, there will be a great historical revival in Myanmar, and Myanmar will be changed into a nation that believes in Christ. I am waiting to see the great things that our Lord God will do soon. I serve him according to his revelations. I thank God for what he has been doing all this time and the good things he has planned for Myanmar.

Glory to God!

RESPONDING WITH PRAYER:

1. Please pray for spiritual breakthrough in Myanmar.
2. Read Isaiah 32:14–16 and pray through these verses for Myanmar.
3. Ask God to reveal to you an area or issue that he is calling you to pray for specifically. Spend time praying for that.

"As soon as the coup happened, I thought I would really hate soldiers and want to swear at them and kill them. But to my surprise, I have not sworn at soldiers even one time, I don't have hatred for them, and I even pray for them to be convicted [persuaded] and turn to the right way. I have learned more through reading Scripture."

—Myanmar national

EDDY

*Noun. A flow of water spinning in the opposite direction
of the main current.*

My name is Rose May Myat. During my first year at university, one senior student in my dormitory gave me a booklet about God's love and plan. From that time on, I was spiritually mentored, and I came to understand the salvation God offers. I came to depend on the power of God. I started to pray and read the Bible, and whenever something challenging happened, I prayed first instead of trying to solve it by myself. As I attended the discipleship training offered by our campus student ministry, I learned how to share the gospel with others.

In my second year, I was able to nurture the first-year students and share the gospel with them. Every year after that, I was able to attend mission trips with the campus ministry team. After graduation, I also served one year as a volunteer with the students' ministry group. After graduation, I planned to go into business. But God had another plan for me, impressing upon me the message in Psalm 2:11, "Serve the Lord with fear and celebrate his rule with trembling." I felt God ask me to serve him in this way. However, no one in my family encouraged me, and I myself didn't want to go into ministry work. Two of my aunts worked as missionaries, and their lives were very difficult. My parents worried that, if I worked in missions, I would suffer as they did. They wanted me to have a small business and live a smooth and easy life. I also worried about these things. But, due to my family's situation and the difficult times our country faced, I came to understand that God had planned and prepared for me to go into the mission field.

Before accepting this opportunity, I felt there was something heavy and blocked inside my heart. Only after I made the decision to serve in his mission did I feel free. God prepared everything for me, despite my own concerns of facing difficulties.

During my ministry training period, I had the opportunity to share the gospel and conduct discipleship training in two villages. Then, with ministry volunteers and staff, we went to some districts in Yangon and were able to conduct more evangelistic work and discipleship training. We were also able to reach out to the students of the medical college, whom we taught and mentored. People seem more open to hearing the gospel than they used to be, though others have started to believe that there is no God.

We are really thankful that we can reach out to people, not only online but also in person. Right now, I am working with other churches to reach out to children of other faiths. I feel very happy when I share the gospel, and God has given me the ability to express his love to others.

May the Lord bless the donors who helped and supported my student ministry.

In his service,
Rose May Myat

RESPONDING WITH PRAYER:

1. Please pray for Myanmar national missionaries. Pray for wisdom and a sensitivity to the Holy Spirit as God leads them in ministry.

2. Have you ever felt challenged or reluctant to do something you believed God was asking you to do? Ask God for a heart that reflects his own and a deeper trust that he will equip and empower you.

FLOW

Noun. The pace and uninterrupted movement of water in a certain direction.

My name is Cung Cung. I graduated with a degree in electrical engineering from a technology university. In my third year, a senior staff member at our university's campus ministry gave me a booklet on God's love and plans. She shared the gospel with me, asking me questions like "Do you really believe in God's love and grace for you?" That question led me to a deeper confidence in who God is and that I can be in heaven with him after I die. Before that, even though I was a Christian, I doubted God's grace and wasn't sure if I would go to hell if I did something wrong. As I trusted God more, I started to depend on him instead of trying to do things or solve problems my own way.

Ministry staff continued to teach us the Scriptures with follow-up lessons and Bible studies. As I came to understand more, I came to depend even more on God's power. I attended basic, intermediate, and advanced Bible study training and also went on mission trips. I learned to share the gospel with others. On the last day of training, there was a call for those willing to become volunteer staff for one year, and I, along with three others, volunteered. After we finished the volunteer training session, there was a call to action challenging us to become full-time staff and attend a new staff training.

Because I am the eldest son in my family, the six years of study it took to become an electrical engineer, and the sacrifices my family made for my education, I felt unable to disappoint my parents. I didn't take up the challenge. Instead, I decided to work as an engineer so I could earn some money and take care of my family with that income. However, while I was at university, I learned more about God and had a burning heart to help people in need of the Lord. Again I learned to trust further in God's power. This all happened because a senior staff member shared the gospel with me and helped me to trust in God's promises. I feel the confidence and joy that salvation assures me. I understand the meaning of his saving grace and feel peace and relief, knowing that I will join him in heaven. So I feel this need to share the gospel with others and help them to know the same assurance and joy I have.

It is also important to know how to be in the right place at the right time. I was of two minds about the path forward—deciding whether to work as an engineer or work for God—so I prayed fervently to God to show me the way. God gave me a reply through 1 Corinthians 9:17, "If I preach voluntarily, I have a reward; if not voluntarily, I am simply discharging the trust committed to me." It was as if God spoke directly to me. So I worked in ministry and took care of my family. By the grace of God, my grandmother who was seriously ill recovered completely.

God has done amazing things for me, too. Amid the political turmoil, and in spite of the danger of traveling, God enabled me to go down to Yangon to attend a full-time ministry-worker training class. I thank God for all that he has done and continues to do.

RESPONDING WITH PRAYER:

1. Please pray for provision for the families of Myanmar national missionaries.

2. How do you define success and security, and what do they look like to you? Ask God to reveal his perspective to you and ask him to redefine what success means in your own life.

RIPPLES

Noun. Small waves resulting from the continued and expanded outward movement of water, resulting from an external force or impact.

My name is Nwe San. Since the year 2000, I have been on the staff of a student-led ministry. I am based in an upper Myanmar town and have been able to reach out to students attending university in other towns in the state. Since 2020, there have been upheavals and a lot of difficulties because of the pandemic and the military coup. In spite of all these challenges, we have been able to see the fruit of our labor in our mission work. I praise God that during these challenging times, he has given us opportunities to reach people, and I see him nurture and change their lives. I would like to share a few of these stories.

One man, Ko Shwe Oo, who works for a large media corporation, was struggling with drug addiction, and his life was in chaos. He came from a Buddhist background, but through Facebook and social media, he heard about God and became interested. He wanted to escape a life of drug addiction and lead a happy, healthy, and normal life instead. He had tried to stop using drugs on his own, but he hadn't been able to do it. Discouraged, he prayed to God, who he had heard could do anything. He said, "If God is really the true God, let me be free from drug addiction, which I can't do with my own strength." God then gave him a mind that loathed drugs, and he no longer wanted to use them.

He had a Christian friend, and one day, the friend took him to church and introduced him to me. I shared the gospel with him, and we talked about the salvation of God and eternal life. He continued his journey with God and began to take part in Bible studies over Zoom with me as well. After discussing it with the pastor of the church, he was baptized on April 17, 2022. His parents and family, though Buddhist, were happy to see the new Ko Shwe Oo, who had escaped drug addiction and was leading a new life. He used to be very short-tempered and easily enraged, but, miraculously, God changed his whole mindset and gave him a mind of patience and endurance.

Another man, Ko Yin Zar, was working with a Christian NGO in its microfinance department. He also came from a Buddhist background. At his organization, all staff are welcome to join devotions in the morning, which he would attend. He heard about God, but he did not believe or accept him—he had his own god, Buddha. One day, Ko Yin Zar had a motorcycle accident and injured his hand. He prayed to God to heal him, and God did. Because of this experience, he had a taste of the living God. He felt and saw God's power through this healing, and he started to learn more about God and the Bible. He welcomed follow-up studies with me to nurture his faith, and he also attended some basic and intermediate Bible-study classes. Together with Ko Shwe Oo, he was baptized on April 17, 2022. He has continued to participate in the Zoom Bible-study program and also takes part in mission activities.

Phyu Lin, a PhD student in philosophy at the university here, comes from a Muslim background. After starting her studies at the university, she began attending church with her friends and became interested in Christianity. Taking part in the worship service gave her a sense of peace and joy. I was able to share the gospel with her and support her burgeoning faith. During the pandemic, she chose to be baptized.

My neighbor, Li Wa, is not from a Christian background, but her grandmother is a Christian. Her grandmother had hoped for her granddaughter to become a Christian minister and serve in ministry. The tenth-grade exam in Myanmar is a critical exam that students must pass in order to move forward with their schooling. Li Wa took this exam and failed—she was very disappointed and wanted to try again and pass the next year. So she went to Naw Bu Baw Prayer Mountain in Karen State and prayed to God to give her the chance to pass the tenth-grade standard exam. That year, she passed the exam, and from this she believed that God is a living God who hears and answers prayers. During the pandemic,

I was able to spend more time with Li Wa and encourage her in her relationship with God. She decided to be baptized in 2021, and her grandmother was able to see the changed life of her granddaughter before passing away.

During these difficult and challenging times, I praise God that he gave me the privilege to introduce Ko Shwe Oo, Ko Yin Zar, Phyu Lin, and Li Wa to Christ. At present, I teach and nurture these four people in their journey with Christ. During this year, I have also seen God's provision in bringing others to help share the gospel. I recruited four new workers who will volunteer in a student ministry for one year. They have completed the three-month volunteer training and work with the staff in evangelism. In addition, one of my students has finished the new staff training, and she is now on staff in one ministry team.

God has also blessed our online activities as we are able to continue with our teaching and Bible study with students who are believers. We have continued to share with students from all backgrounds about God's love and blessings. We also work in participation with other churches with young believers.

I pray that God will continue to bless us in our mission work.

Lovingly,
Miss Nwe San

RESPONDING WITH PRAYER:

1. Please pray for people in Myanmar who are hearing about Jesus. Pray for his love to take root in their hearts and grow into a deep and meaningful relationship with him.

2. How can you build trust with people in your life who don't yet have a relationship with Jesus? Ask God for wisdom and guidance in how to come alongside them.

WELLSPRING

Noun. A bountiful and sustaining source of fresh water.

"Before I formed you in the womb I knew you, before you were born I set you apart; I appointed you as a prophet to the nations."
—Jeremiah 1:5

First of all, I would like to thank God that I can share my testimony. My name is Saw Kaung. I completed Bible school in 2007, and in 2008, I began participating and helping in my church. During the COVID-19 pandemic in 2020, I started to work as a minister of Christ in the village where I am living now. I thought that it was a good time to preach the gospel and share the love of God, since most people were facing challenges. I believed I was chosen by God to be a minister. At first, I gathered a few believers and some nonbelievers together and started a worship program. In 2020, I was so happy that God made a way to celebrate the first Christmas in our village, which included mostly nonbelievers. This was a special blessing because most villages could not celebrate due to COVID-19.

In 2021, I formed a committee with believers and nonbelievers to build a church. The military did not allow people to construct new buildings, and they oppressed minority groups in particular. Because of this, I was especially thankful to God for holding my hand and leading me forward with full strength in the construction of the church. With him, I could overcome everything in the midst of all of the conflict and criticism as well as financial, political, and security crises. On December 28, 2022, we held a worship program for the Christmas celebration and the completion of the church. Looking back at this situation, it's clear that everything was God's work.

In the current political situation, I am especially thankful to God for allowing me to provide spiritual, physical, and educational support to children and youth in the village as well as outreach to the elderly. Even though I hear the sounds of war every day, by the grace of God, I am given the opportunity to minister in the midst of difficulties. I cannot do anything myself, but I know that God can do everything.

The verse Jeremiah 1:5 is about God redeeming me. I put all my heart, intelligence, and strength into God's hands so I can continue my life's journey. I believe that God will use me even more in the future. My prayer and hope is to be used by God more, to accomplish the plans that he has set, and to work with the Holy Spirit as a missionary.

My favorite scripture as a minister is Proverbs 3:5–6: "Trust in the Lord with all your heart and lean not on your own understanding; in all your ways submit to him, and he will make your paths straight."

I would like to conclude with this Bible verse. May God bless all who read this testimony.

RESPONDING WITH PRAYER:

1. Please pray for Christians in Myanmar who are in environments that are hostile to their faith. Please join this author in prayer, that he may effectively partner with the Holy Spirit in ministry.

2. The author mentions Proverbs 3:5–6. How does that verse speak to you in your life now? Take time to pray through that.

"Before, I didn't give the Holy Spirit a chance in my life, so I did not hesitate to do things God didn't like. Now I let the Holy Spirit lead my life, and he guides my life step by step. Therefore, I am sharing my testimony that giving the Holy Spirit the chance to lead us means that, as Christians, we can easily do everything we could not do and be able to live in the glory of God. God bless all of you who read this."

—Myanmar national

FOR DEEPER REFLECTION:

1. The authors of these stories seem to go to great lengths to share the gospel with others, even through the current crisis. They have sacrificed careers, plans, family approval, safety, the ability to live in Myanmar, means of income, and many other things. What do you think drives them, and why do they choose to make these sacrifices? What are the honest emotions or thoughts these examples stir in you?

2. What differences do you see in sharing the gospel when comparing these stories from Myanmar to your own culture? What can we learn from them? How might these examples inspire you?

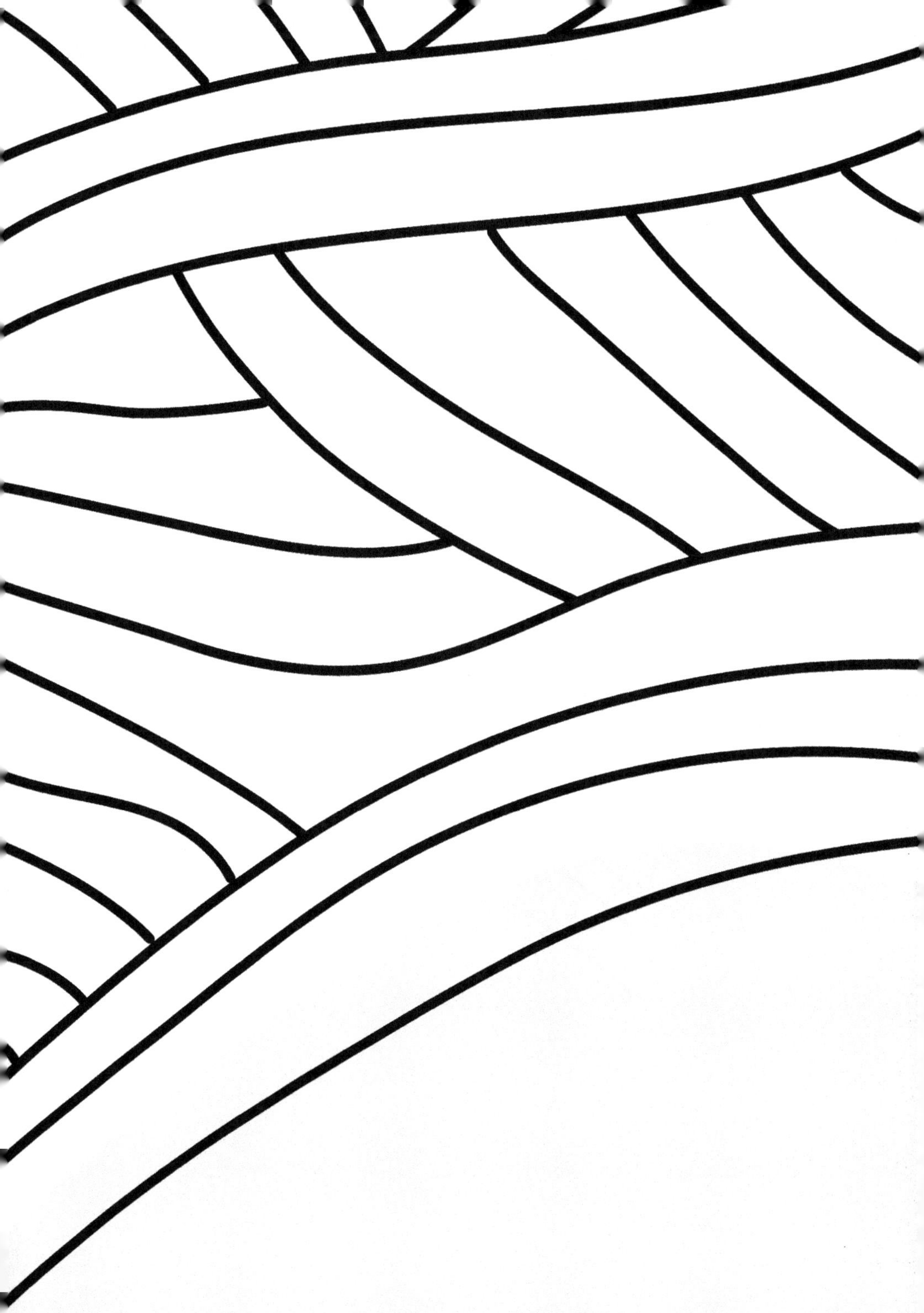

EDGES

Noun. The precarious points of rocky outcrop, as in a canyon or cliff; a perilous or hazardous environment that threatens impending catastrophe.

> He opened the rock, and water gushed out; it flowed like a river in the desert.
>
> —Psalm 105:41

"Moving to another country is different from living in our own country. After I arrived in Thailand, I felt like I was under house arrest. On the way to the market one day, I was arrested by the Thai police. I had to follow them to the police station. If I wanted to be released, I had to pay the money that they asked for. I didn't have any money to pay them. By the grace of God, I was released without paying any money to the police—I called some of my friends to help me, and with their help, I was released. Starting from that day, I didn't dare go outside at all, so I stayed in the house. I didn't even dare go out to the market to [buy food to] cook, and I had to buy and eat what was sold in front of my house.

After living in Thailand for a long time, the money that I had ran out. Also, I couldn't find a job due to not having the legal documents to stay in Thailand, and I had no income. At that time, I felt so stressed and anxious. The challenge of living in a country that isn't my home is being afraid of everything and living with worry. By the grace of God, I can still stay and live in Thailand. Without God, I believe that I would have been arrested, and I wouldn't have food to eat because I have no job or income. But because of God's love and grace, I can still eat, and I don't feel hungry. So far, I am safe from the police too."

—Myanmar national

"If I [didn't] blindly trust in God, I would be a fool. He is the only hope I have, and I will go on continually putting my faith in him."

—Myanmar national

TORRENT

Noun. An immediate, abrupt surge of water that inundates.

One experience I would like to share is when we ran away from the war. Before the conflict, I worked in my village with my parents, harvesting beans, sesames, and peas, and I also worked temporary day jobs with my aunt. In addition, I participated in charity work in my village.

One night, I had to flee to another place because we heard that fighting would break out the next day in the village I was in. The following morning, we heard that there was going to be a real war. I had never experienced anything like having to run away because of a war or an incoming plane before, and I was terrified. The village I ran to after fleeing my own had a water shortage and no electricity or phone lines. If we wanted to use our phones, we had to go to the top of the mountain, and even then, we could not always connect to phone service. If we wanted to bathe fully, we had to walk to the river. I was very depressed because I was alone and away from my family, and I was filled with anxiety.

But as he promised, God did not forsake his children. We had to run away from the war with only one item of clothing, but God prepared clothes and everything for us. Through our friends and a Christian organization, he provided clothes, food, and other things we needed.

Since God created us and knows all things, he knows what his children need, how we are feeling, and what we are facing every day. Therefore, in the Bible, in Matthew 6:31–32, we are told not to worry about how to eat and how to dress because God is our Creator, and he knows what we need for our bodies, minds, and souls. In Philippians 4:19, it says, "And my God will meet all your needs according to the riches of his glory in Christ Jesus." When we believe in Jesus Christ, we are God's children, so we must believe that God will provide everything his children need.

We must rely on God. God has spoken and provided through the Bible, my friends, and teachers for the needs of my body, mind, and soul.

Even today, God protects and supports us. No matter what kind of difficulties we face, we can overcome everything if we are with Emmanuel, God who is always with us, and God who never forsakes us. Our God is good all the time to us. Thank you all. Just trust in God, rely on God, and hope in God. God bless you.

RESPONDING WITH PRAYER:

1. Philippians 4:19 says, "And my God will meet all your needs according to the riches of his glory in Christ Jesus." Please pray for the needs of internally displaced people in Myanmar to be met, including food, water, shelter, and means of communication.

2. What needs do you currently have in your own life? Ask God to reveal to you how you can strengthen your trust in him to meet your needs.

SUBMERGE

Verb. To remain fully encompassed by water.

First of all, I would like to praise and give thanks to God. God is good to me. May the name of Jesus be glorified forever and ever.

I can share my testimony because of Jesus in my life. I was a traditional Christian. If I'm speaking truthfully, I was a Christian because my parents were Christian. I didn't know about Jesus. I just thought that if I got baptized, I would go to heaven when I died. So I got baptized. However, because I knew about God but didn't accept God in my life, I was under the power of pride. I did all kinds of unhealthy activities, like drinking alcohol, doing drugs, and gambling, even though I am a girl, and these things are especially unacceptable for women in my culture. I married a nonbeliever, and I started to believe that God didn't actually exist.

However, God is very loving. No matter how much I rejected him, he never rejected me. By the grace of God, I faced a terrible disease in my life, and the doctors could not save me. It was like receiving a death sentence. People forget God when they are in good health, but they remember God when the time comes to die. We are afraid to die, and we are afraid of what might happen afterward. Because of this, I felt like I saw God for the first time. No one could save me, but I believed that God could save me. At that time, I confessed all my sins and apologized. When I approached God with true regret, he listened to my prayers.

1 John 1:9 says, "If we confess our sins, he is faithful and just and will forgive us our sins and purify us from all unrighteousness." I prayed to God, "Please let me live so that I can find you. I want to serve you." God answered my prayers. I had prayed that if God would save me, I would serve in ministry and live for God. I have not fully recovered from the disease, but I am healthy, and I am serving in a ministry and living for God. God showed himself faithful, so now I want to show my faithfulness by serving him.

Jesus is the most essential thing in my life.

John 14:6 says, "Jesus answered, 'I am the way and the truth and the life. No one comes to the Father except through me.'" According to this scripture, I can share the testimony of God's goodness to people through Jesus, who is the truth.

May God bless all who hear this. Amen.

RESPONDING WITH PRAYER:

1. Please pray for people in Myanmar suffering from chronic diseases.

2. The author says she knew about God but didn't accept him in her life and that this led to a prideful attitude. Are there areas in your life where you're aware of God's perspective but haven't allowed him to work? Take time to ask God for a spirit of humility.

DELUGE

Noun. An enormous overflow of water with a time of extended reach.

My name is Tarni. I live with my family, and I have two lovely daughters. I had a chance to work in an anti-human trafficking program for an international nongovernmental organization (NGO), and I would like to share how God worked in this project. Part of our program provided services to assist trafficking survivors or family members of trafficking survivors according to their needs and requests. These services included liaising and working with local and anti-trafficking police. If necessary, we went to police stations and judicial offices. When I went to these places, I saw aggressive people, people in despair, and people in grief. I felt very grateful to God for his protection and guidance for me and my family members.

During this project, I handled four cases: two cases involving the rescue of survivors and punishment of the perpetrators, one case involving the rescue and return of survivors back to their hometown, and one case cooperating with the Philippines police to rescue a survivor. When we received this case about a Myanmar citizen being trafficked in the Philippines, it was not a good time due to the pandemic and the political unrest in our country. Many government workers were part of a civil disobedience movement (CDM), and our program and the national office were also in the final stages of closing.

After thinking carefully, I prayed and asked for God's help. I remembered the Bible verse that says our God is called "Wonderful Counselor, Mighty God" and can do miracles, and Psalm 37:5, "Commit your way to the Lord; trust in him and he will do this." I received peace and strength by declaring those verses. Everything went smoothly except for some language challenges with the survivor's family members, as they were from another ethnic group. Our organization and another international organization had offices in both Myanmar and the Philippines, which greatly helped with coordination for rescue, repatriation, and reintegration. I don't believe this was a coincidence; I totally trust that this was God's work.

According to the survivor, the traffickers were cruel enough to kill their captives with little provocation, and he told us the best time and method to organize a rescue. He emphatically asked us not to use other ways because he had seen the traffickers beat and torture another victim who tried to run away. We carefully communicated this to the other agencies and were all waiting anxiously at the arranged time. Then I got a message from the victim saying, "Why didn't you do what I said? The traffickers know that I plan to run away. They will try to move me to a different location. They told me that they will kill me." Possibly, because there were many agencies involved in the rescue, one had moved forward in a way that contradicted the victim's directions. As soon as I read the message, I prayed to God, "Lord, help him and prove what you can do. Redeem this situation. I absolutely trust that you can do an impossible thing at this impossible time. As you parted the Red Sea and changed water into wine, please make a miracle in this case too."

After two days, I got a message from my organization's office in the Philippines that they had rescued the victim successfully. We were able to safely return him back to his family within two months. As I myself have experienced God's powerful hand and seen amazing things by trusting his word with all my heart and declaring it with my mouth, I would like to encourage others with my testimony. This is all. I pray that you, the reader, may also feel God's joy and peace.

RESPONDING WITH PRAYER:

1. Please pray for Myanmar people who are currently in situations of human trafficking or have returned home from situations of trafficking.

2. Think of a time when you were in an unsafe or challenging situation and God provided a way out. Take time to thank him for his rescue and protection.

PARTED

Adjective. An unnatural movement of water dividing to create a path forward.

I would like to share how amazingly God protected my brother's life. Due to the civil war in our town after the coup, my parents and brothers had to run away to another village. They had previously run a clothing store and a grocery shop in our town, but they started a business selling rice and petrol in the village they fled to. One day, on the way back to the village after buying rice and petrol from town, the military arrested my brother and his traveling companions and seized all of their goods, taking three trucks and nine people. All of the civilians were tied with their hands behind their backs and had to sit with their faces to the ground. They could not raise their heads at all.

The soldiers confiscated all the goods on the trucks. They commanded the drivers to take the trucks to the soldiers' station, and the remaining civilians were brought through a forested road as hostages. The soldiers threatened that if there were any gunshots or explosions on the way to the station, they would kill everyone. All the hostages were forced to walk in a straight line so that if the soldiers decided to kill them, they could kill them easily.

When my brother and others in the group arrived at the station, they saw a corpse with a bamboo spike through its neck. Junior soldiers sharpened bamboo in front of the group and threatened to kill them with the sharpened spikes if anyone did not listen to what they said. At night, the soldiers tied people's feet in pairs so they could not run away. The group had to bow their heads the whole night. One person tried to stretch his neck as he had become very stiff, and all of the soldiers kicked and hit him.

The junior soldiers sharpened their knives, cut bamboo, and constantly threatened to kill the hostages. My brother only focused on their leader. He listened to what the leader reported to his supervisor about the group—what goods they brought, how many people there were, and other related information. My brother paid attention to what the leader did and prayed in his mind the whole time, telling God, "If I die now, I will leave my parents with debts, and my family members will not be able to bear the burden. But if you think it is time for me, your will be done." God listened to his prayer.

At night, the leader unexpectedly came and talked with my brother. Having been rude to my brother from the start, he became surprisingly friendly. He asked about my brother and his family. He told my brother that he would report to his leaders about the group, and if his leaders agreed to let them go, they would free them all, but if the leaders said to finish them, they would all be killed. By the grace of God, the leader received orders to release them. In the morning, he also gathered all the goods and phones his soldiers had confiscated from the group and gave them back to my brother. He even paid back the cost of the stolen rice.

Before my brother's group was stopped, two other trucks had been detained. They were destroyed, and all of the people and goods were set on fire. My brother's group saw the aftermath, including the scorched earth and the charred remains of clothing and bones. Walking past this horrific scene, my brother understood how close to death he had been and felt how good God was to him.

We witnessed that with God, an enemy became a friend. The sudden change in the lead soldier's attitude was inexplicable. God is good. God not only loves my brother but also loves us, and he listens to our prayers.

Family members of people in my brother's group thought that they had all been killed, and they had already held funeral receptions and services. But how good is our God! Everyone in my brother's group was freed and returned safely. I cannot describe how joyful it was to reunite with them. My brother shared his testimony, saying that without God, he would not have survived. The only reason he could be free was by the grace of God.

For me, I can't even begin to describe the goodness of God. Everything good that happens is because of him. I have come to the conclusion that without God, we are nothing. Please be encouraged by this testimony of God's goodness in our lives.

> **RESPONDING WITH PRAYER:**
>
> 1. Please pray for Myanmar people who have been kidnapped, threatened, arbitrarily arrested and detained, or kept as political prisoners. Please also remember their families in prayer.
>
> 2. Think of people in your life who have caused you pain. Ask God to soften your heart toward them and show you how to pray for them.

"God is good all the time. He drew me closer during this crisis, and he makes me stronger. I used to worry so much about the small things . . . but God changed me, and now I'm able to encourage others—physically, mentally and spiritually—through this crisis."

—Myanmar national

LIFELINE

Noun. A descriptor of water that characterizes it as fundamental for continued life.

"Even though I walk through the darkest valley, I will fear no evil, for you are with me; your rod and your staff, they comfort me."
—Psalm 23:4

First of all, may God's grace be upon everyone. We are able to live each day of our lives because of God's guidance. I would like to testify about something I experienced that I will never forget, through the daily experience of God's grace.

The experience I would like to share happened when I was a seventh-grade student. In December, all the Christian teachers from my school gathered all the students, and everyone celebrated Christmas together. After worshiping, they planned to feed all the people who came to the celebration, including the students, with Karen traditional food (clam *tarlapot* and fish paste). The seventh-grade students went to the river to collect the clams. Although some students swam while they were collecting the clams, one of my friends and I stayed on land because we couldn't swim. When there was no one around, I slipped and fell into the water. I began to drown. At that time, the whole world went dark for me, and I finally stopped struggling. I was so confused. I started to pray to God, but before I could finish, everything went calm, and I lost consciousness.

When I woke up, I was standing near the water's edge. Everything had happened quickly, but it felt like a long time to me. I was on the shore again. I tasted God's grace in that moment, and it was an unforgettable experience. What I know is that I am not alive today because of human efforts. It is only because of God's grace.

RESPONDING WITH PRAYER:

1. Please pray for people in Myanmar to see more undeniable examples of God's power at work.

2. Has there been a time where you or someone you know has experienced God's power? Take time to thank him for that and ask him to help you see more of him in your life.

WATERFALL

Noun. A powerful and compelling flow of falling water.

My name is Saw Eh Doe. I was born in Southeast Myanmar, and I am the oldest of six siblings. I was baptized in my local church when I was eighteen years old. I got married in March 1988, when I was twenty-six. In the month after my marriage, not only did the church elect me as a deacon, but I was chosen as one of the four cupbearers to share the bread and wine during the church service. I tried to learn from the elders as I was young and lacked education.

Because that year was a time of crisis and protests,[1] our region faced severe war. Village administrators were killed frequently in our area, so no one dared become an administrator. At that time, most of the village administrators who worked for the military were being killed by resistance groups for being informants. Because we had no administrator in our village, it was under various pressures from the government.

The military administration threatened the villagers, insisting they choose a village administrator to control the military administration system, but no one wanted to take that responsibility since the villagers did not support the military. Even though the village elders also sat in meetings every day, they were facing difficulties because there was no designated administrator. Finally, they decided to let the decision fall to chance. They each drew pieces of concealed paper to see who would draw the piece that contained the administrator role. One old man from the village drew that piece of paper, meaning the role of the administrator would fall to him. After the meeting, the

---

[1] *The "8888 Uprising" that began on August 8, 1988, marked a powerful statement from Myanmar nationals against the Myanmar military and signaled a call for democracy. What followed was a violent crackdown from the Myanmar military across the nation in an attempt to quell the voices of its country's people.*

old man went back home with a sad expression. When he arrived at home, he went upstairs without saying anything to his family and tried to kill himself. Noticing the sadness in her husband's face, his wife went upstairs soon after and was able to stop him in time. The wife knelt and begged the elders in the village to reverse the decision, then shared her husband's story with them.

At that time, I had already started serving as a deacon in the church. I knew that if the villagers had to relocate to avoid repercussions from the military, our church would also have to move and would face difficulties. Therefore, I volunteered to be the administrator to prevent the destruction of the village. Some elders of the church rejected my offer, saying that a church deacon should not be the administrator. However, no one could solve the problem of not having an administrator, so the church allowed it. When I started working as the administrator, I called the village elders and asked them to pray for me and dedicate me to God. Whenever a situation seemed unclear, decisions were made with the prayers of the village elders.

The conflict between the resistance group and the military was quite intense. The military thought that the village administrators were not cooperating with them, and they started tracking down the administrator for our village. Many ethnic group leaders had already been killed because the military thought they were supporting the resistance. One day, a villager came to me and said that I should no longer be the administrator, and I should leave the village as soon as possible. I made preparations as quickly as I could and went to another village to hide. While I was hiding, some of our friends, who were administrators in other villages, were killed. When the military came looking for me and I was not there, some villagers were detained and locked in the school. They were told that they would stay in the school until they died if they didn't get the administrator to come back. If the administrator didn't show, the military would burn the villagers to death. In the evening, one of the elders of the village took pity on the villagers. He signed a pledge that he would be the administrator, and the villagers were able to go home.

About a week after I heard the news, I returned to the village because there was a new administrator in my place. After arriving at the village, I slept at my home, and at five o'clock the next morning, the military came and arrested me. About two hundred villagers and I were arrested and forced to sit on the road. Six soldiers waited with us, and the rest left. After a while, the ethnic armed group that the Myanmar military was in conflict with started shooting at the soldiers. The soldiers shouted at us not to run and directed us to crouch on the side of the road. I also shouted at the villagers to obey the soldiers' orders but to also pray to God. I did the same, reciting Psalm 46. The soldiers used us as human shields to prevent getting shot at by the resistance group, and about two hundred people were caught in the close-range crossfire, which included five shotguns and one heavy weapon, for about half an hour. I thought many of the villagers would die. However, when the battle was over, no one was hurt; only one villager's toe was slightly injured. I was astonished. When I tell this story, some people might think it is impossible. However, the two hundred villagers who faced the incident with me are also witnesses. That day, March 27, 1989, was Armed Forces Day,[2] when God gave me the greatest testimony of my life.

After the battle, when it was calm, the soldiers returned and set fire to my village. They burned down twenty-two of the thirty-nine houses, and all the barns, chickens, and pigs were destroyed. In May, after the destruction, a small preschool was built from bamboo for the children. One day, a military captain came to my village and asked what it was, and I told him it was a preschool. Out of spite, he said he would make the structure even smaller. After twenty-eight years, God provided the means to build a great and beautiful church and hall on the preschool's grounds—the exact place that the captain said he would make smaller. After I went through this incident, I believe that there are things people can't do, but there is nothing God can't do. He shows himself whenever we need him. Therefore, may our beloved brothers and

---

2 *Armed Forces Day, celebrated annually in Myanmar on March 27, commemorates the people's resistance to Japanese occupation during World War II.*

sisters take strength from Psalm 46 and from my testimony. God bless you all. Amen.

PSALM 46

God is our refuge and strength,
an ever-present help in trouble.
Therefore we will not fear, though the earth give way
and the mountains fall into the heart of the sea,
though its waters roar and foam
and the mountains quake with their surging.
There is a river whose streams make glad the city of God,
the holy place where the Most High dwells.
God is within her, she will not fall;
God will help her at break of day.
Nations are in uproar, kingdoms fall;
he lifts his voice, the earth melts.
The Lord Almighty is with us;
the God of Jacob is our fortress.
Come and see what the Lord has done,
the desolations he has brought on the earth.
He makes wars cease
to the ends of the earth.
He breaks the bow and shatters the spear;
he burns the shields with fire.
He says, "Be still, and know that I am God;
I will be exalted among the nations,
I will be exalted in the earth."
The Lord Almighty is with us;
the God of Jacob is our fortress.

RESPONDING WITH PRAYER:

1. Please pray for breakthrough and conviction in the hearts of the Myanmar military.

2. In what areas of your life or in society have you noticed history repeating itself in painful ways? Take time to pray for breakthrough in those harmful patterns.

EVERFLOW

Noun. A never-ending and reliable flow of water, fed by a deep and abundant source.

I was born in Myanmar, and I live for Christ. On August 14, 2019, I received a revelation while praying. I saw a map of our country, and I was told to go around the country and pray for every state and region. After doing this, I saw that the map became bright and shining. I asked God more about this. He told me that it was not enough to pray in my room or in a building—it was important to walk on the land in each state and region and pray because there was an evil bondage and foundation in Myanmar that was already rooted into the ground.

By the grace of God, I was able to organize a prayer group committed to traveling to and praying for states and regions. After further prayer and revelation, it became clear that there were two main objectives in this prayer movement: first, to remove darkness from his church and any dark strongholds in the Christian community. Secondly, it was to remove darkness outside the church, to lift the shadow from people's eyes, minds, and hearts, so that when they heard the gospel, they could welcome a life-giving relationship with Jesus.

Through these revelations, I came to understand that God wanted me to focus my efforts on the spiritual realm and not on the physical realm. Later, I thought back on this time and time again at the height of the COVID-19 pandemic and during the military coup.

In September, we started the prayer movement in Yangon, and each month the Lord would show me, with confirmation from our prayer group, which state or region would be the next destination. None of us would know in advance which place would be next, but the Holy Spirit would reveal it in a picture or word. Sometimes the destination would be a place we had never been to before, or it was a small town, but it would be a representative place of that state and region. If the Holy Spirit did not reveal the next destination, we would wait until he did.

We made sure to pray and ask for confirmation each time the next location was revealed. After the COVID-19 pandemic began in 2020 and then the military coup in 2021, it became very dangerous to travel. We wanted to be sure that God was calling us to each specific place.

The calling of the Lord is very powerful, and despite the political upheaval and my family's objections, God's grace compelled me to go. I know that my family voiced their concerns because of their love for me, but I also know that the Lord loves me more. I always asked God, "Please demonstrate Your love and reveal Your presence so people will know that You are with me, and that this is being done according to revelation from You." He did not fail—from the beginning to the end of each journey, God held us securely in his hands.

When we went to Chin State, we were called to a town in the Chin hills. There is one road that can be used to travel there, and it is very narrow and winding. This road continuously experiences armed conflict as the military tries to send troops through it while resistance groups seek to impede their advance by ambushing them. By God's grace we were able to arrive at the town safely, even though we were stopped and questioned at army checkpoints. We were an unlikely group of travelers, given the circumstances—for this trip, there were only three of us women.

In addition, because of the distance as well as the security risks, it was expensive to travel to this town. However, the Lord provided everything for us—one church took responsibility for our transportation and provided a driver and a car. The Lord also inspired one rich man in the town to provide for our hotel and meal costs. Finally, the Lord prepared a prayer committee from Chin State to meet with us there. About fifteen pastors from the township's prayer committee met with us to pray in church together, and it was a powerful time. Most of the pastors and ministry leaders were crying as they felt the love of God during prayer. They also said they felt God's demonstrated love through the action of three women, traveling from Yangon to this town in the midst of active conflict. We told them we were simply obeying what God had told us to do. They felt so cared for and encouraged when they understood that the Lord had chosen their state and town. He had not forgotten them, and we praised God together.

When we tried to leave the town, the military stopped our car along with a passenger bus. We heard that there was fighting again on the road, and since the road was so narrow, it would not be possible to turn around even if we were caught in live gunfire. As I was the trip leader, my companions asked me what we should do. During this time, we also received a phone call from the rich man asking us to stay back in town for the night due to the conflict on the road.

But the Lord had already shown me the trip ahead of time. He had confirmed to me in a vision that we would arrive safely at a town along the way where we would spend the night. We would hear huge explosions before completing the rest of the trip to Yangon safely. I prayed again to God and asked if we should go. I looked out the window, and God revealed huge angels to me—they were incredible and as tall as mountains. I was confident that he was confirming his protection over us, and I let my companions know. About ten minutes later, our car was permitted to slowly move forward, and we were finally able to continue our journey. By the grace of God, we did not meet any conflict on the way, and we arrived safely at the town where we planned to stay overnight.

After dinner at the hotel, I suddenly heard deafening explosions that shook the building. The explosions were like nothing I had experienced in Yangon—they were so much louder, so much closer. Even though God had let me know about this before, I felt stunned. Our family members called and messaged us, as they had heard about the outbreak of fighting in that town and knew we were there. We reassured them that we were safe and arrived back in Yangon the following day, unharmed.

During later trips, I gained a deeper understanding of the spiritual battle over Myanmar. The Holy Spirit showed me that evil had established foundations in Myanmar; however, the Lord had destroyed the foundations of Satan. He told me that in the spiritual realm, he had already arrested all of the evil spirits, and he would build his church instead.

On one trip, the Holy Spirit directed me to go to two towns; however, none of my prayer partners were able to accompany me during the first part of the journey. I was discouraged on the plane, and I told the Lord, "You always send me with companions, but now I'm alone." I asked him to help me. He then opened my eyes to see two angels, one on my left and one on my right—they were crystal clear and shiny, incredibly beautiful and tall. They accompanied me the whole flight, and I felt their presence for the rest of the trip.

Finally, I met with a prayer partner after arriving in the first town. We traveled from this town to the second town, which crossed contested territory between the military and resistance fighters. The closer we came to the second town, the more ill I started to feel. My head felt cloudy and dizzy. When we reached the hotel, I collapsed. I asked my traveling companion to pray for me, and I took medicine. One of our prayer partners called, asking if I was okay, because she had felt compelled to go into intercessory prayer for me. Again I asked the Lord to open my spiritual eyes to see what was happening, and again he showed me. I saw huge warrior angels fighting against the area's territorial evil spirits, who had high authority, dominion, and power. But the Lord's angels always win. I slept that night, and although it is not my culture's common practice to do so when feeling sick, I felt inspired to take a shower in the morning. I felt that the Lord cleansed me from head to toe, and I was released from the pain and felt refreshed.

We did not have access to any means of transportation, but we felt called to walk the town and pray, so we walked. Each time we entered a shop for water or purchased fruit from a vendor along the way, we shared the gospel with those we met. While we walked, I saw the glory of the Lord in front of us, which looked like fire, and it also covered us from behind. What I observed during this trip was that no one noticed us—it was as if the Lord covered us with his wings so we could freely walk and speak with people. It did indeed feel that God had arrested darkness and opposition. When we felt that God told us it was finished, we returned to the hotel.

Within a week of our return from this trip, it felt like the devil got very angry and attacked us—both my companion and I were in separate motor vehicle accidents within a short span of time. However, by the grace of God, we were protected and not harmed; only her motorcycle and my car were damaged.

After we returned to Yangon, there was an earthquake in the town we had just left. A famous idol statue was destroyed, its head shaken off and smashed. We have heard reports that the gospel is now reaching many people in this area, which was so resistant to the gospel before. One church out of Yangon has now been able to establish a church in each city of Myanmar, and many people have accepted Christ.

> **RESPONDING WITH PRAYER:**
> 1. Please pray for believers in Myanmar to have renewed and increasingly deeper relationships with God.
> 2. Is there anything you have placed above God in your life? Ask God to help you prioritize him.

"Whenever I feel down or sad, I take strength from Isaiah 41:10: 'So do not fear, for I am with you; do not be dismayed, for I am your God. I will strengthen you and help you; I will uphold you with my righteous right hand.' We can see God's promise in the verse that HE is on our side, and HE will strengthen us and support us with his faithful right hand.

No matter how bad situations are, if God is on our side, we can overcome everything and succeed. No matter how many failures and sorrows there are, there is God who will always give strength and comfort. God's hand is always there to help and support us. Therefore, walk with God only by faith. God always keeps his promises."

—Myanmar national

FOR DEEPER REFLECTION:

1. What thoughts or emotions do these personal accounts of miracles trigger in you? Do they challenge or inspire you in any way?

2. How might we be prevented from seeing or experiencing miracles in our lives?

3. Do you ever hesitate to ask God to do miracles or answer big prayers? If so, why?

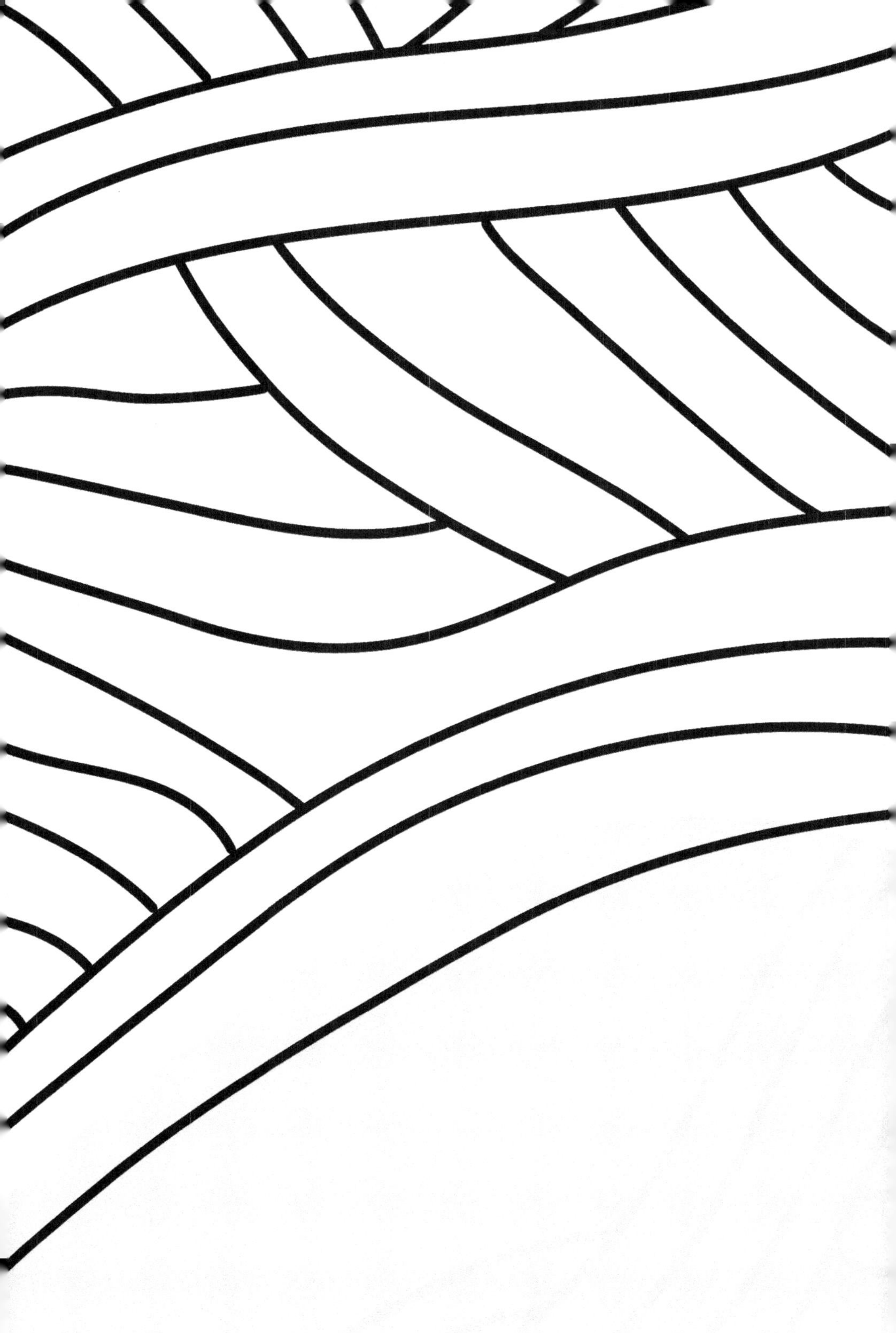

NOTE TO MY FIRST LOVE

Have you ever missed someone you love even when they are sitting or standing beside you?
I have. Even though I am walking in the path of His grace daily, I miss Him.
I look at the birds, the sky and the clouds, the flowers and leaves; they remind me of Him so much, His goodness and unfailing love which are as beautiful as the nature I am witnessing.
The times I was really frustrated, He waited for me like a lover till I got over my anger and showered me with His love again.
When I felt lonely and abandoned, He sent out birds from the west part of the world to the desert where Israelites were wandering to give them meat, He sent out people from east, west, north, and south to show how much He cares for me through them.
I learned about people who found You near the end period of their lives, but
God, I am so grateful to have found You as my first love.
Oh God, I miss You.

—D. R. Par

DELTA

Noun. A fertile land formed over time through the deposit of sediment.

I remain confident of this: I will
see the goodness of the Lord in
the land of the living.

—Psalm 27:13

"I want to share that we need to live with God. This is very important. We must hear the voice of God and follow Jesus. Even if we don't have anything, that's okay. With the Word of God, everything is complete. I was very depressed and wanted to forget. The Word of God strengthened me and reminded me that we already have the victory so we don't need to forget, and I can walk with God again."

—Myanmar national

"I put my trust in God. As a human being, what I can do is limited. The situation may seem hopeless—it may be something I never dreamed I would face—but it is nothing compared to Jesus dying on the cross for us."

—Myanmar national

RAIN

Noun. Water falling from the sky, reaching large swathes of land at one time; a welcome reprieve during times of drought.

One week before the coup, our prayer network committed to forty days of prayer with partial fasting. Feeling led by the Holy Spirit, I fasted and prayed for an additional three days. During that time, the Holy Spirit showed me a picture of a map of Myanmar, which was then split into two parts. One part disappeared, while another part totally collapsed. Eventually, the map was totally gone. I didn't understand this picture, and I continued to seek guidance from the Lord.

Finally, the Holy Spirit revealed to me the meaning of the picture—it was showing that the Lord planned to do a new thing in Myanmar. He wanted to recreate the country's foundations and make them brand new. I was led to Isaiah 43 in Scripture.

I believe it is our role as followers of Christ to intercede for the nations, to dispense grace, to pray for those who harm us and for their freedom from evil, and to entrust God with vengeance instead of seeking retribution ourselves.

I would like to encourage my Christian brothers and sisters to lean on and find their hope wholly in God. Our prayers matter—I have seen that when there is breakthrough in the spiritual realm, there is breakthrough in the physical realm. I have also seen that God wants to work intimately with us and through us—spiritual battles happen in partnership with our active, prayerful participation. When the situation seems to get worse, we need more prayer.

There can be pain in the waiting, but that doesn't mean nothing is happening. In Jeremiah 29, God says that he knows the plans he has—we don't know, but he knows. He is trustworthy even when we feel depressed. He is trustworthy even when we want revenge. He is trustworthy even when the world is on fire.

Let us trust him, no matter what the situation.

> **RESPONDING WITH PRAYER:**
>
> 1. Meditate on Isaiah 43.
>
> 2. Please pray for God to bring restoration and revival to Myanmar.
>
> 3. Are there areas in your life where you feel like you're painfully waiting? Ask God to remind you that he is still doing something in the waiting. Ask him, in his grace, to give you a glimpse of what he is doing.

"My favorite Bible verse of all time is Matthew 6:33: 'But seek first his kingdom and his righteousness, and all these things will be given to you as well.' My mom also always taught me to read the Bible and pray regularly and to tithe every time I got pocket money. To seek his kingdom first and to tithe consistently was always in my mind, but sometimes I still couldn't give my tithe regularly. Since I was inspired by a story I had heard about a successful and faithful businessman who tithed more than 40 percent of his income, I decided to be faithful with giving tithe and have been doing it without fail ever since. I can see that God keeps his promises in my life and has always provided everything that I need. God is good and faithful all the time."

—Myanmar national

"Bring the whole tithe into the storehouse, that there may be food in my house. Test me in this,' says the Lord Almighty, 'and see if I will not throw open the floodgates of heaven and pour out so much blessing that there will not be room enough to store it.'" —Malachi 3:10

CASCADE

Noun. The successful, falling progression of water as it advances through stages.

First, I pray that you will receive the joy that comes from God, good health, and all blessings according to God's will.

My name is U Tin Aung, and I worked at an international nongovernmental organization (NGO) for three years. It was a Christian humanitarian organization. I want to praise God because I arrived at that organization through God's guidance.

I was a nominal Christian before. I didn't walk with God and did not participate in his work. I did not seek God's presence and did not rely on God. I lived as I liked, and I enjoyed worldly things. That's how I avoided God all my life. As I grew older, I didn't notice that my spiritual life was very weak. While changing jobs one after another, I was far away from God. At one point, I was unemployed for almost two years, and none of my efforts helped me to get a job. At that time, I was driving a taxi for a living. That was not my dream job, and I was depressed and disappointed. I began to think I was useless because no one wanted to hire me. I felt like God had left me.

I worked when I wanted to work. If I wasn't feeling good, I didn't work. I lost control, and I lost hope. I decided to surrender to God and trust him. I had faced a lot of trouble, and I approached God again. I prayed that he would bring me closer to him. I put my job in God's hands. I relied on God and hoped for his help as I continued to search for a job.

Finally, I went to Singapore to look for work. However, even after one month, I still hadn't found a job, so I returned to Myanmar. One year later, I found a job advertisement from this Christian organization, and I applied for it. I had applied for that job once before, and I did not get it, so this was the second time I applied.

At the same time, I was finally offered work in Singapore. I did not know which job I should choose, so I prayed to God. I prayed that my heart would be strengthened and that I would desire to participate in the work that would bring me closer to God. I made the decision to reject the job offer from Singapore even though I did not know for sure if I would get the job at the Christian organization. God made a way for me, his lost son.

One month later, by the grace of God, I received the good news that I was hired at the Christian organization. When I went to work, I met God's people, who were really amazing. They were truly pure-hearted and humble colleagues who actively worked to serve God. Before starting our work every morning, we entered into God's presence, giving thanks and seeking his will in a morning prayer program. It helped me know more about God's goodness.

My colleagues' testimonies and the encouragement of God's word brought me closer to him. It made my heart never want to stray from God. I could thank God for everything. I could learn to trust and listen to God in every situation. When I surrendered my heart to God, I found peace in my life.

Matthew 11:28, which says, "Come to me, all you who are weary and burdened, and I will give you rest," was right, and it was fulfilled in my life.

Dear friends, what burden are you carrying in your life? Is it a job? Is it health? Is it livelihood? If you can't fix it yourself, don't despair. Put it in God's hands. Remember that God can do all things. God will give you peace and depth of life. I am currently serving as the second financial holder at my church. I have also decided to participate as a local preacher. Even though I went my own way, God uses me in his work because of his great love and his plan.

I want you to believe that God has great love and a great plan for you. I pray for all of you readers to receive God's joy, peace, and hope in your life. Amen.

RESPONDING WITH PRAYER:

1. Please thank God for each author, their heart posture towards him, and their ministry to you.

2. Take time to ask God to use the accounts in this book to encourage you and remind you of his personal love for you.

"Even in the midst of crisis and political instability, remember that God is sovereign and in control. Take comfort in knowing that his plans are greater than any human circumstance. Trust in his wisdom, seek his guidance, and find strength in his promises. Through faith, we can endure, persevere, and overcome. Let not your heart be troubled, for God is with you, and he will make a way where there seems to be no way."

—Myanmar national

FOR DEEPER REFLECTION:

1. How have the stories in this book impacted you? What are your takeaways? How has the Holy Spirit been speaking to you throughout these stories?

2. This book defines "desert river" as a place of God-shaped life, growth, and change in the midst of desolation. How can you be intentional about looking for desert rivers in your own life?

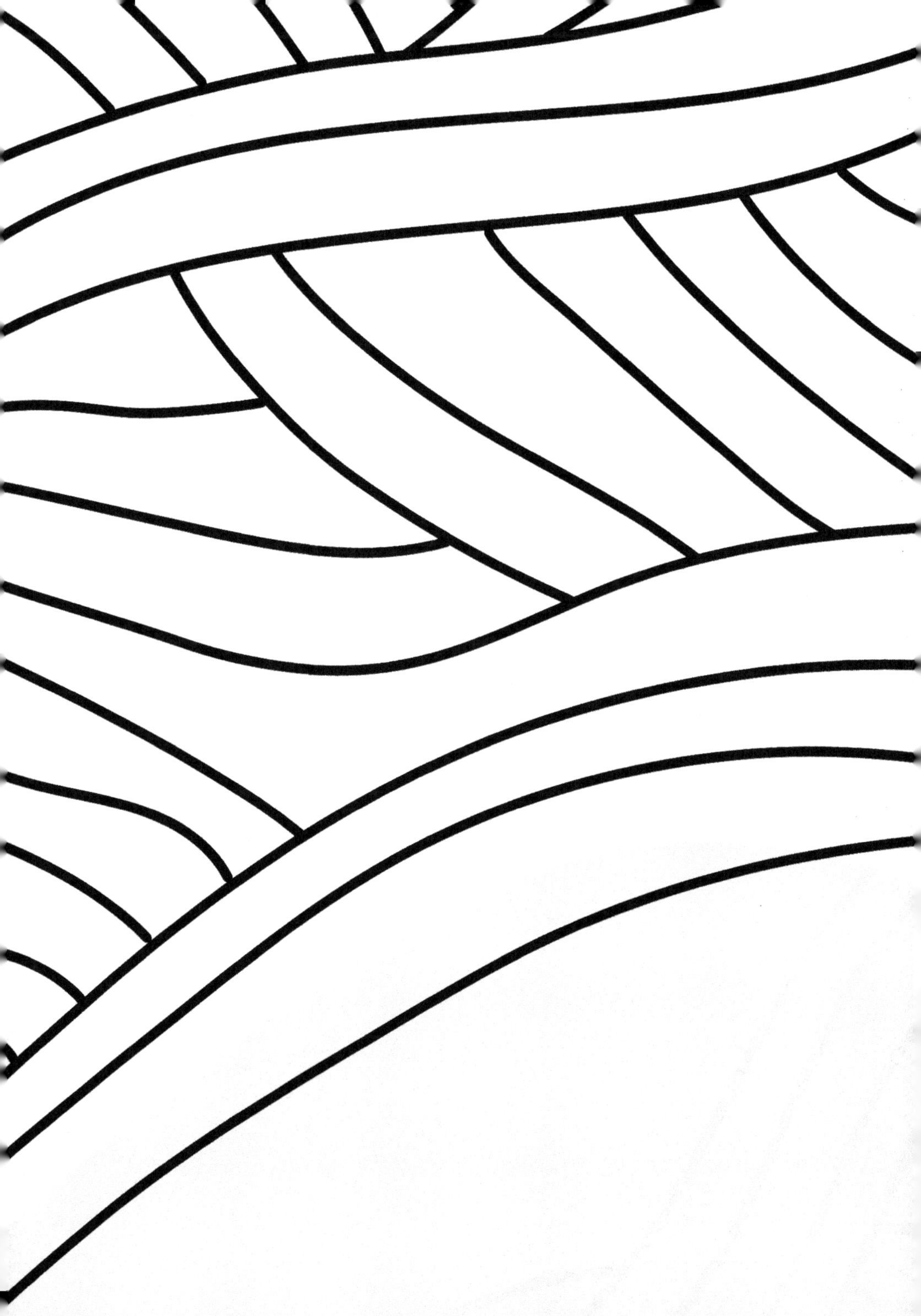

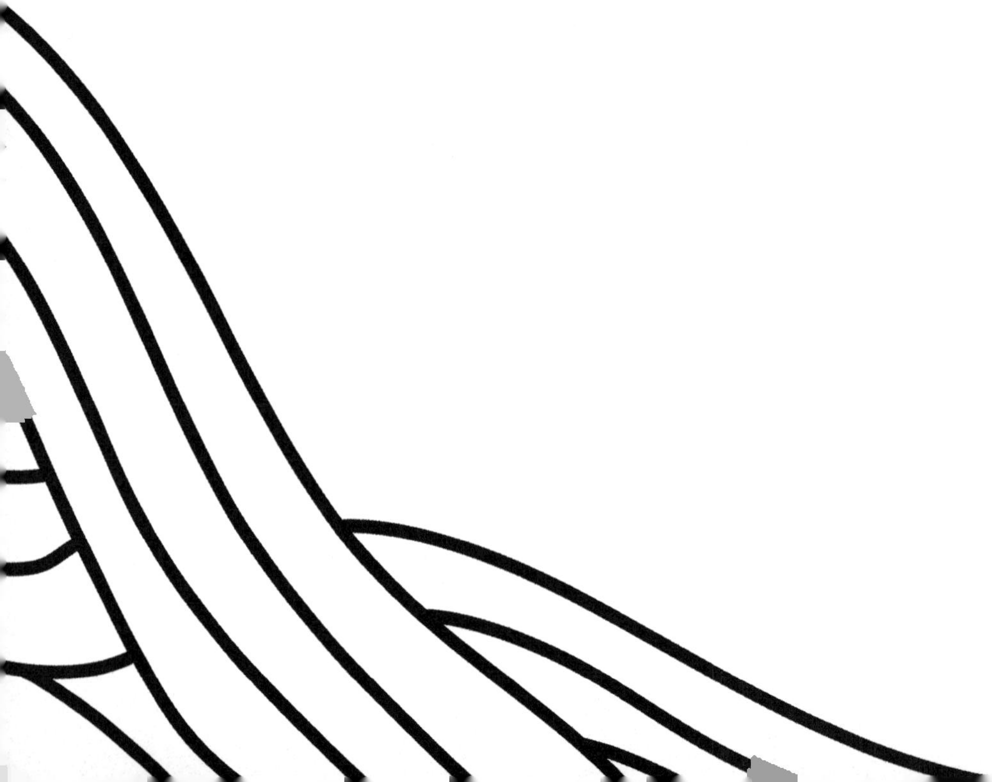

GOD IS GOOD

Even in the face of suffering, God is good
HE saved me from suffering
Even in the face of sorrow, God is good
HE makes sorrow become joy
Even in the face of difficulties and problems, God is good
HE gives the answers in the midst of difficulties and problems
Even in the face of failure, God is good
HE makes failure become success
No matter what the situation is, God is good
God who is above all situations is always good.
God is good all the time.

—Su L. N.

CONCLUSION

Throughout this book, we have heard from the young and the old, from students, mothers, doctors, migrants, pastors, seamen, IDPs (internally displaced people), and refugees. These stories have been submitted from across the country in Myanmar, from urban sprawls to villages and IDP camps. We have heard from believers across denominations, family backgrounds, financial situations, and ethnicities. We have been witnesses to stories of healing, deliverance from death, guidance from God's Word, raw lament, and the simple but beautiful obedience to sharing hope in Jesus. The common uniting theme in these stories has been the recognition and worship of God in the midst of crisis, be it through personal accounts, poems, expressions of grief, or declarations of faith that rail against despair.

We know that the penning of these stories has involved tears, heartache, and exhaustion for the authors interviewed for this book, even in the midst of joy and celebration for what God has done. We deeply thank them for sharing the most formative and vulnerable parts of their story with us—and, in turn, with you.

For our editorial team, we have personally lingered on the implicit question for ourselves: what does this mean for us? Do we really believe God is who he says he is, which may appear contrary at times to the things that we see, experience, or feel—or the lack thereof? When we are surrounded by clouds of encroaching doubt and confusion, can our trust in him be reclaimed—and if so, how? Do we believe that a river is somehow there—created for us, a lifeline for us—in the midst of the wasteland?

We find ourselves absorbed by these authors who, at the time of writing, are still in the midst of chaos and war. They keep asking for his presence and provision again and again. Even when the situation doesn't seem to change—even in the continued anguish of loved ones dying, life savings lost, family homes destroyed, homelands scorched—they come back. They are determined to come back. The cynical part of our hearts considers that foolishness. The God-breathed part finds it compelling.

We hope that these stories have profoundly impacted and encouraged you as they have impacted and encouraged us. We hope that they give you pause to reflect on how God has been present in your life as well, even when it all seems to be falling down.

Please continue to pray for Myanmar—for revival, for God's kingdom of peace and justice, and for breakthrough in the violence.

Thank you for taking the time to read this book and these stories told by believers in Myanmar about how they have seen God's rivers in the desert.

We know there are many more stories to tell.

Because he hasn't stopped, and he won't stop now.

WHAT'S NEXT?

Thank you so much for purchasing and reading this book in support of Myanmar. We hope that these stories have encouraged you and connected with your mind and heart.

It can be difficult to know how to support and stay connected with Myanmar Christians across the world, so we have provided some suggestions below for those who feel inspired to further action.

1. Please Tell Others

We would really appreciate your support in spreading the word about this book to others. Is it possible to share this with your church, ministry, small group, network, family members, or friends? Would this book be an appropriate gift for anyone in your circle? As all proceeds from book sales will be sent back to Myanmar to support communities in need of shelter, medical supplies, food, clean water, and other basic necessities, your support will help increase the scale of aid that can be provided. To see updates on how funds have been used to reach those in need of humanitarian assistance, please visit our website, everflowmyanmar.weebly.com; connect with us on Instagram, @desertriver_myanmar; or find Desert River on Facebook.

In addition, if you enjoyed this book, please leave us a review and/or rating on Amazon, as it will help others find the book and hear about why it can be worth the read. You can also email us at everflow.myanmar@gmail.com.

2. Please Pray

Your prayer support is invaluable. To download a free seven-day prayer guide on Myanmar, written with Myanmar believers, please go here: https://everflow.aweb.page/7dayprayerguide-Myanmar. The guide will be emailed directly to you and can be used for small groups, family prayers, and/or independent prayer time. We deeply believe that God works powerfully through prayer, and we thank you for your spiritual investment in Myanmar.

3. Please Connect

Please also consider sending us encouraging messages for Myanmar believers at everflow.myanmar@gmail.com. We will re-share those encouraging comments on our Facebook page, where believers can read and hear about how you have been praying for them, how their stories have impacted you, and/or how you have taken action to support them in this time of crisis.

Finally, we have also included links on our website for more information on the situation in Myanmar and providing support, and we welcome you to explore these resources.

From the bottom of our hearts, thank you so much for partnering with us in thanking God for what he has done and continues to do, and for supporting communities across Myanmar.

ABOUT EVERFLOW

We are a group of eight like-minded volunteers who believe that God is still active and moving in Myanmar. Six of us are from Myanmar, one is from America, and one is from Canada. It is our aim to thank God for his faithfulness and to see those in Myanmar affected by war supported physically and spiritually. We are excited for the proceeds from this book to return to Myanmar to assist with humanitarian needs. While we have worked hard to record, curate, organize, edit, design, and share this book, it could not have been possible without the sacrifice and generosity of the authors. To our authors: we hope that you see Jesus within the pages of this book, just as you've seen him in real life.

Thank you for entrusting your story to us. Thank you for sharing your desert river.

Printed in Great Britain
by Amazon